OCCASIONAL PAPER 179

Disinflation in Transition, 1993–97

Carlo Cottarelli and Peter Doyle

INTERNATIONAL MONETARY FUND

Washington DC

1999

Production: IMF Graphics Section
Figures: Sanaa Elaroussi and In-Ok Yoon
Typesetting: Victor Barcelona

Cataloging-in-Publication Data

Cottarelli, Carlo.
Disinflation in transition, 1993–97 / Carlo Cottarelli and Peter Doyle.,—
       Washington, DC : International Monetary Fund, 1999.
        p.   cm. — (Occasional paper, ISSN 0251-6365 ; no. 179)

    "Issues in Transition"—Cover.
    Includes bibliographical references.
    ISBN 1-55775-797-6

    1. Monetary policy—Europe, Eastern.   2. Monetary policy—Europe,
Central. 3. Monetary policy—Former Soviet Republics. 4. Inflation (Finance)—Europe, Eastern. 5. Inflation (Finance)—Europe, Central.
6. Inflation (Finance)—Former Soviet Republics.   7. Economic stabilization—Europe, Eastern.   8. Economic stabilization—Europe, Central.   9.
Economic stabilization—Former Soviet Republics.
10. Industrial productivity—Europe, Eastern.   11. Industrial productivity—Europe, Central.   10. Industrial productivity—Former Soviet Republics.   I. Doyle, Peter.   II. International Monetary Fund.
III. Occasional paper (International Monetary Fund) ; no. 179.
HG930.7.C67 1999

Price: US$18.00
(US$15.00 to full-time faculty members and
students at universities and colleges)

Please send orders to:
International Monetary Fund, Publication Services
700 19th Street, N.W., Washington, D.C. 20431, U.S.A.
Tel.: (202) 623-7430   Telefax: (202) 623-7201
E-mail: publications@imf.org
Internet: http://www.imf.org

recycled paper

Contents

The following symbols have been used throughout this paper:

. . . to indicate that data are not available;

n.a. to indicate not applicable;

— to indicate that the figure is zero or less than half the final digit shown, or that the item does not exist;

– between years or months (e.g., 1994–95 or January–June) to indicate the years or months covered, including the beginning and ending years or months;

/ between years (e.g., 1994/95) to indicate a crop or fiscal (financial) year.

"Billion" means a thousand million.

Minor discrepancies between constituent figures and totals are due to rounding.

The term "country," as used in this paper, does not in all cases refer to a territorial entity that is a state as understood by international law and practice; the term also covers some territorial entities that are not states, but for which statistical data are maintained and provided internationally on a separate and independent basis.

Preface

This Occasional Paper, another in the series on special issues in transition, reviews the experience of disinflation during 1993–97 in Central and Eastern Europe and in the Baltics, Russia, and other countries of the former Soviet Union. Inflation dropped dramatically during this period, with the Baltics, Russia, and other countries of the former Soviet Union catching up with earlier progress made in the early 1990s in many Central and Eastern European countries. This paper reviews the economic policies that were behind the decline in inflation as well as other factors that facilitated the process.

The authors of this paper, Carlo Cottarelli and Peter Doyle, are both members of the European I Department. Their work greatly benefited from the cooperation provided by desk economists working on transition countries in both the European I and European II Departments. They also would like to thank for their helpful comments Gerard Belanger, Michael Deppler, John Odling-Smee, Oleh Havrylyshyn, and Tom Wolf. Helpful suggestions were also received from Executive Directors to whom a previous draft was presented at a Board seminar. The authors are also indebted to Patricia Emerson and Indra Perera for assisting in numerous drafts, to David Maxwell for research, and to Martha Bonilla of the External Relations Department for editing the paper and coordinating its production and publication.

The opinions expressed are solely those of the authors and do not necessarily reflect the views of the IMF, Executive Directors, or the authorities of the countries covered in this study.

I Introduction

Almost all transition countries experienced an initial spike in inflation at the outset of the reform process as price controls were removed. The speed of the subsequent disinflations, however, varied markedly, partly reflecting the different times when countries gained monetary and political independence. Some Central and Eastern European (CEE) countries had managed to reduce inflation to the two-digit range already by the end of 1992, while inflation remained close to or above 1,000 percent in the Baltics, Russia, and other countries of the former Soviet Union (BRO). Subsequently, inflation continued to fall gradually in the Central and Eastern European countries, albeit with some notable exceptions. But it fell sharply in the Baltics, Russia, and other countries of the former Soviet Union, where, by the end of 1997, it exceeded 100 percent only in one country. As a result, median 12-month inflation in the whole transition group fell from 950 percent at the end of 1992 to 11 percent at the end of 1997.

This paper focuses on the experience during 1993–97 of 10 Central and Eastern European countries and the Baltics, Russia, and other countries of the former Soviet Union. It reviews a range of policies implemented in transition economies through the prism of their contribution to disinflation, and factors that were particular to the transition context.[1] The paper is organized as follows. Section II outlines the recent inflation and output record. It notes that inflation peaked at higher rates, the output collapse was more marked, and disinflation came later in the Baltics, Russia, and other countries of the former Soviet Union than in the Central and Eastern European countries. Nevertheless, output began to recover within two years of successful disinflation in both areas. Section III discusses the econometric evidence concerning the links between inflation and output. No general evidence is found that disinflation compounded other factors depressing output, but evidence is found that the moderate and low inflation environment brought about by disinflation stimulated growth. Section IV attempts to identify the factors that facilitated such apparently low-cost disinflation, including the transition context in which disinflation occurred and the role of fiscal policy. Section V discusses the experience of coun-tries that, having successfully reduced high inflation, remained in a moderate inflation range for several years. Section VI summarizes the findings and draws out the implications for the inflation rates that transition countries should target in the years ahead.

---

[1]The disinflations in Central and Eastern European countries during 1990–92 have been discussed in Bruno (1992).

II Inflation Developments

By the end of 1992, major results in stabilizing inflation had been achieved only in the Central and Eastern European countries: inflation had dropped below 60 percent in the Czech Republic, Poland, and Slovak Republic (Table 1).[2] Hungary

had always remained well below this threshold.[3] Inflation in the ruble zone was high and rising at this time. It surged dramatically in many countries that

---

[2]The term "inflation stabilization" is used here to indicate a stable decline of inflation below the 60 percent threshold (see footnote 1 in Table 2 for a more precise definition). While this threshold is arbitrary, few countries that managed to break it experienced

major inflation reversals. Moreover, the results discussed in this review are quite robust to the choice of the threshold. The term "disinflation" is instead used to indicate the overall process of reduction in inflation, including in the poststabilization period.

[3]This partly reflects its gradual price liberalization during the 1980s and, in comparison to some transition countries, its generally cautious monetary policy in that period and thereafter.

Table 1. Twelve-Month Inflation Rates in Transition Economies
(End of period)

	1992	1993	1994	1995	1996	1997
Albania	236.6	30.9	15.8	6.0	17.4	42.1
Bulgaria	79.4	63.8	121.9	32.9	310.8	578.6
Croatia	937.3	1,149.7	−3.0	3.7	3.5	3.9
Czech Republic	12.6	18.8	9.7	7.9	8.6	10.1
Hungary	24.7	21.1	21.2	28.3	19.8	18.4
Macedonia, FYR	1,935.0	241.9	55.0	9.0	−0.6	2.7
Poland	44.5	37.7	29.5	21.6	18.5	13.2
Romania	199.2	295.5	61.7	27.8	56.9	151.6
Slovak Republic	9.1	25.0	11.7	7.2	5.4	6.4
Slovenia	...	22.9	18.3	8.6	8.8	9.4
CEE median	79.4	34.3	19.8	8.8	13.1	11.7
Armenia	1,241.2	10,896.1	1,884.6	32.1	5.7	21.8
Azerbaijan	...	1,291.6	1,788.1	84.5	6.7	0.4
Belarus	1,561.5	1,995.0	1,957.3	244.2	39.1	63.4
Estonia	942.2	35.7	41.6	28.8	15.0	12.3
Georgia	1,335.1	7,543.8	6,471.6	57.4	13.7	7.3
Kazakhstan	2,960.7	2,172.6	1,157.6	60.5	28.6	11.3
Kyrgyz Republic	1,257.0	766.9	95.7	32.3	34.9	14.7
Latvia	958.2	34.9	26.5	23.6	13.5	7.1
Lithuania	1,162.5	188.8	45.0	35.5	13.1	8.5
Moldova	2,198.4	836.8	115.9	23.8	15.1	11.1
Russia	2,321.6	841.6	202.7	131.4	21.9	11.0
Tajikistan	...	7,346.3	1.1	2,135.2	40.6	163.6
Turkmenistan	...	...	1,328.6	1,261.5	445.9	21.5
Ukraine	2,005.0	10,153.6	401.1	181.4	39.7	10.1
Uzbekistan	910.0	885.0	1,281.4	116.9	64.4	50.2
BRO median	1,296.1	1,088.3	401.1	60.5	21.9	11.3

Source: IMF staff estimates.

Table 2. Disinflation Thresholds[1]

	Peak Inflation (1990–97)	Peak Inflation Date	Stabilization Program Date[2]	Months To	Inflation<60	Months To	Inflation<30	Months To	Inflation<15	Months To	Inflation<7.5
(Countries that stabilized before 1993)											
Czech Republic	67.6	1991, June	1991, Jan.	3	1991, Apr.	1	1991, July	2	1991, Oct.	2	N/A
Hungary	31.0	1995, June	1990, Mar.	N/A	N/A	N/A	N/A	N/A	N/A	N/A	N/A
Poland	1,173.0	1990, Feb.	1990, Jan.	18	1991, June	33	1994, Dec.	21	1996, Oct.	7	1996, Dec.
Slovak Republic	73.7	1991, June	1991, Jan.	3	1991, May	1	1991, June	2	1991, Oct.	46	1995, Sep.
Slovenia	88.2	1992, Dec.	1992, Feb.	N/A	N/A	3	1992, Oct.	27	1995, Feb.	N/A	N/A
(The 1993–97 stabilizations)											
Albania	336.8	1992, Oct.	1992, Aug.	5	1993, Feb.	3	1993, May	23	1995, Apr.	2	1995, July
Armenia	29,600.9	1994, May	1994, Dec.	6	1995, June	10	1996, May	N/A	N/A	N/A	N/A
Azerbaijan	1,899.0	1994, Nov.	1995, Jan.	5	1995, June	1	1995, Aug.	7	1996, May	7	1996, Dec.
Belarus	2,809.6	1994, Aug.	1994, Nov.	9	1995, Oct.	11	N/A	N/A	N/A	N/A	N/A
Bulgaria (1st stabilization)	304.5	1992, Jan.	1994, Dec.	3	1995, Mar.	N/A	N/A	N/A	N/A	N/A	N/A
Bulgaria (2nd stabilization)	2,040.4	1997, Mar.	1997, Apr.	6	1997, Oct.	N/A	N/A	N/A	N/A	N/A	N/A
Croatia	1,944.9	1993, June	1993, Oct.	4	1994, Feb.	1	1994, Mar.	2	1994, May	0	1994, May
Estonia	1,241.9	1992, Sep.	1992, June	18	1993, Dec.	8	1994, Aug.	23	1996, July	N/A	N/A
Georgia	50,654.0	1994, Sep.	1994, Sep.	3	1994, Dec.	17	1996, May	1	1996, July	N/A	N/
Kazakhstan	3,033.3	1994, June	1994, Jan.	17	1995, May	13	1996, June	11	1997, May	N/A	N/A
Kyrgyz Republic	1,257.0	1992, Dec.	1993, May	23	1995, Apr.	24	1997, May	N/A	N/A	N/A	N/A
Latvia	1,444.6	1992, Nov.	1992, June	9	1993, Mar.	27	1995, June	12	1997, June	11	1997, June
Lithuania	1,412.6	1992, Nov.	1992, June	21	1994, Mar.	26	1996, May	2	1996, July	N/A	N/A
Macedonia, FYR	2,100.3	1992, Oct	1994, Jan.	6	1994, June	8	1995, Feb.	5	1995, July	5	1995, Dec.
Moldova	2,198.4	1992, Dec.	1993, Sep.	9	1994, June	9	1995, Mar.	14	1996, June	N/A	N/A
Romania	317.0	1993, Nov.	1993, Oct.	9	1994, July	N/A	N/A	N/A	N/A	N/A	N/A
Russia	2,321.6	1992, Dec.	1995, Apr.	9	1995, Dec.	5	1996, June	N/A	N/A	N/A	N/A
(Countries that did not stabilize)											
Turkmenistan	2,669.1	1996, Oct	N/A	N/A	1997, Mar.	3	1997, June	N/A	N/A	N/A	N/A
Ukraine	10,155.0	1993, Dec.	1994, Nov.	18	1996, May	1	1996, June	11	1997, Apr.	N/A	N/A
Uzbekistan	1,936.0	1994, Sep.	1994, Nov.	N/A	N/A	N/A	N/A	N/A	N/A	N/A	N/A
Tajikistan	7,343.7	1993, Dec.	1995, Feb.	N/A	N/A	N/A	N/A	N/A	N/A	N/A	N/A

Sources: National authorities; IMF, *International Financial Statistics*; and IMF staff calculations.

[1]Periods between thresholds were defined using the annualized three-month inflation rates. When these first fell below a threshold, **and** remained there for a year, **and** if the 12-month inflation rate fell below that level during the following year without rising above it again in that year (except for countries in which inflation fell below the threshold during 1997), the country was deemed to have crossed the threshold.

[2]From Fischer, Sahay, and Végh (1996), except for Turkmenistan and Bulgaria.

exited the ruble zone and established independent currencies and new central banks thereafter.

A new wave of stabilization efforts followed during 1993–94 and enjoyed considerable success: during 1993–97, 19 other transition economies managed to break the 60 percent inflation threshold (Table 2)—in most cases without reversals—and by the end of 1997, 16 countries had brought inflation below 15 percent (Table 1). Georgia is a particularly dramatic case, reducing 12-month inflation from 50,000 percent during 1994 to single digits in 1997.

While many countries delayed inflation stabilization for several years—with a relative cluster of stabilizations in late 1994–early 1995—inflation stabilization, once undertaken, was usually rapid. In many cases, less than six months elapsed between the initiation of a major stabilization effort and quarterly annualized inflation falling below 60 percent on a sustained basis (Table 2).[4] Only five countries (Estonia, Kazakhstan, the Kyrgyz Republic, Lithuania, and Ukraine) took about 18–24 months from the beginning of the stabilization to get below 60 percent.[5]

But after the initial inflation stabilization phase, further disinflation was often slow. After breaking the 60 percent disinflation threshold, inflation persisted at moderately high levels (the 15–60 percent range) for more than two years in a number of countries. This slower disinflation group includes the same countries that reached 60 percent slowly (except Ukraine), though Latvia and Albania, which had quickly reduced inflation to 60 percent, joined the group thereafter. However, the most often-quoted cases of persistently moderate inflation (see Cottarelli and Szapáry, 1998) are given by a number of advanced transition economies where inflation had dropped below the 60 percent threshold before the end of 1992. These include Poland (where it took more than four years to bring inflation down from 60 percent to below 15 percent), Hungary (where inflation was still over 18 percent at the end of 1997), and Slovenia (where inflation remained in the 15–30 percent range for over two years after the initial stabilization). Inflation in the Czech Republic and Slovakia has remained stuck to close to 10 percent for a number of years. The median inflation rate of those Central and Eastern European countries that began stabilization before 1993 fell from 27½ percent in 1993 to 15½ percent in 1997; the median inflation rate in the Baltics, Russia, and other countries of the former Soviet Union meeting the same criteria declined somewhat more rapidly, from 35½ percent to 12 percent over this period. Only Croatia and the former Yugoslav Republic of Macedonia have maintained inflation in low single digits for a number of years.[6]

Despite this persistent moderate inflation, the relapses into high inflation were relatively rare (Table 1). During 1993–97, there were three major reversals of inflation after initially successful stabilizations: Bulgaria and Romania in 1996, and Albania in 1997 (Table 1). And Albania and Bulgaria have since renewed their stabilization efforts. While outside the period covered by this paper, the resurgence of inflation in Russia during the summer of 1998 is also notable: the 12-month inflation rate jumped from less than 6 percent in July to 59 percent in October (following a monthly inflation rate of almost 40 percent in September), reflecting the depreciation of the ruble during August 1998. As discussed below, this resurgence of inflation shares many of the features characterizing the relapses into inflation observed during 1993–97.

---

[4]The stabilization initiation dates adopted by Fischer, Sahay, and Végh (1996) have been used to construct Table 2. Most stabilization dates coincide with the starting date of an arrangement with the IMF. When multiple attempts were made (as occurred in six of these countries), "the most serious attempt" was taken. Fischer, Sahay, and Végh stress that the judgment about the seriousness of the stabilization program was not based on eventual inflation performance, but rather on an evaluation of the policy package associated with the stabilization effort.

[5]The marked volatility of inflation throughout the transition area is reflected in findings that lagged inflation has been relatively unimportant in explaining inflation in transition economies (Cottarelli, Griffiths, and Moghadam, 1998; and Coorey, Mecagni, and Offerdal, 1998).

[6]The upward biases in inflation measurement identified by the Boskin report for the United States may be larger in transition economies, given the faster rate of introduction of new products and the proliferation of new retail outlets (Škreb, 1998). On the other hand, lagged adjustments of the weights for goods subject to administered pricing tend to cause inflation to be understated when administered prices rise relative to market prices.

III Disinflation, Output, and the Current Account Balance

Disinflation occurred while output was collapsing, and was often followed by large deteriorations in the external current account balance. This section discusses the links between these developments.

Disinflation and Output Growth

The sharp output drop that accompanied some of the early disinflations led some commentators to voice concerns about the additional output costs that could be associated with fast disinflation (Calvo and Coricelli, 1992; Portes, 1993; Amsden, Kochanowicz, and Taylor, 1994; and Fedorov, 1995). Other commentators, however, have subsequently noted that, as inflation stabilized, growth resumed, often within two years (Figure 1), thus suggesting that disinflation was a condition for sustainable growth (Fischer, Sahay, and Végh, 1996; and De Melo, Denizer, and Gelb, 1997).[7] These two views are not, of course, inconsistent—the former focusing on the transitory costs of disinflation, the latter on the long-term relationship between inflation and growth— and they underscore the complications in assessing the relationship between inflation and growth from simple indicators. These complications are particularly apparent in a period of deep structural changes affecting potential output: the drop in output may have been due to the collapse of central planning, rather than to disinflation, while the recovery may have been due to the effect of structural change, rather than to the stabilized inflation environment.

Only a few studies conduct formal tests of the relationship between inflation and growth for transition economies and they draw somewhat divergent conclusions. Lougani and Sheets (1997) find that, controlling for progress with transition reform (as well as other variables), output growth is negatively affected by inflation: a country with 500 percent inflation in one year loses about 2 percentage points of GDP the following year and 4 percentage points of GDP in the longer run. This finding is echoed by Berg and others (1998) who find different effects of inflation on the private and public sectors: whereas doubling inflation is associated with a decline of 5–15 percent in private sector output, it is associated with increased state sector output by about half that magnitude. They suggest that the latter arises because subsidies to state-owned firms boost their output, but also stoke inflation by raising the fiscal deficit. Thus, they conclude that the impact of inflation on output depends on the relative shares of the private and public sectors. Åslund, Boone, and Johnson (1996) find no significant role for inflation in determining output once both war-torn and ruble-zone dummies are included.

These studies, however, share two main shortcomings. First, they do not investigate whether the relation between inflation and growth may vary at different inflation levels—though there is increasing evidence of this pattern for nontransition economies. Second, they shed no light on the output costs of disinflation, namely whether the change in inflation, rather than the level of inflation, has implications for output. In background work for this paper, Christoffersen and Doyle (1998) address these issues, using panel data on 22 of the 25 transition countries reviewed here (see Appendix I). They find evidence of an inflation threshold for transition economies at about 13 percent: inflation above that level reduces output growth, while no significant effect on growth is apparent if inflation is below that level. They also find no evidence of generalized output loss owing to disinflation.

It is notable that the inflation threshold appears to be higher than that found in market economies (see Appendix I). This suggests that the threshold may be

---

[7]The "transition index" referred to in Figure 1 and elsewhere is drawn from various European Bank for Reconstruction and Development (EBRD) transition reports and from De Melo, Denizer, and Gelb (1997). It is a composite of scores for eight institutional characteristics, ranging from privatization to price liberalization to banking reform and interest rate liberalization. The eight scores are weighted together to yield the aggregate "transition index" for each country. The highest scores indicate institutional structures similar to those prevailing in fully fledged market economies.

Figure 1. The Baltics, Russia, and Other Countries of the Former Soviet Union and Central and Eastern Europe—GDP Growth, Inflation, and Transition Index

(In chronological and disinflation time)[1]

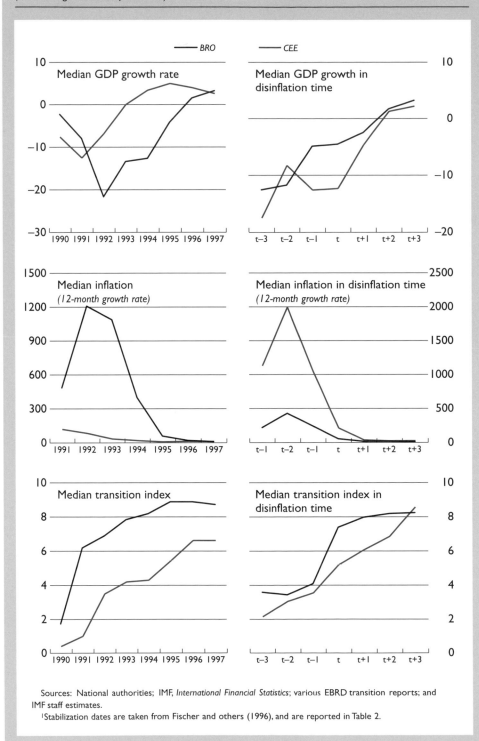

Sources: National authorities; IMF, *International Financial Statistics*; various EBRD transition reports; and IMF staff estimates.

[1]Stabilization dates are taken from Fischer and others (1996), and are reported in Table 2.

falling in transition time, implying that the threshold is lower for the advanced reformers than for the panel as a whole. More specifically, Christoffersen and Doyle (Chapter IV, p. 29) note that inflation may have played a role in facilitating the large growth-enhancing relative price changes at the outset of transition, offsetting other negative effects of inflation on growth. But with structural reforms and the largest of the initial relative price adjustments completed, these initial benefits from inflation would decline, and the relationship between inflation and output in transition economies would come to resemble that of long-established market economies more closely. Thus, the net benefits from low inflation may increase as transition deepens.

In summary, there is evidence that low inflation boosts growth, even after controlling for structural reform and for an inflation threshold that may fall over time as structural reform proceeds. Such a decline in the threshold would be consistent with findings in Fischer, Sahay, and Végh (1996) and Cottarelli, Griffiths, and Moghadam (1998) that fast reformers have, ceteris paribus, lower inflation rates. No clear evidence of a high output cost of disinflation has been found.

Figure 2. The Baltics, Russia, and Other Countries of the Former Soviet Union and Central and Eastern Europe—Current Account Balance, in Percent of GDP, 1990–97
(In disinflation time)

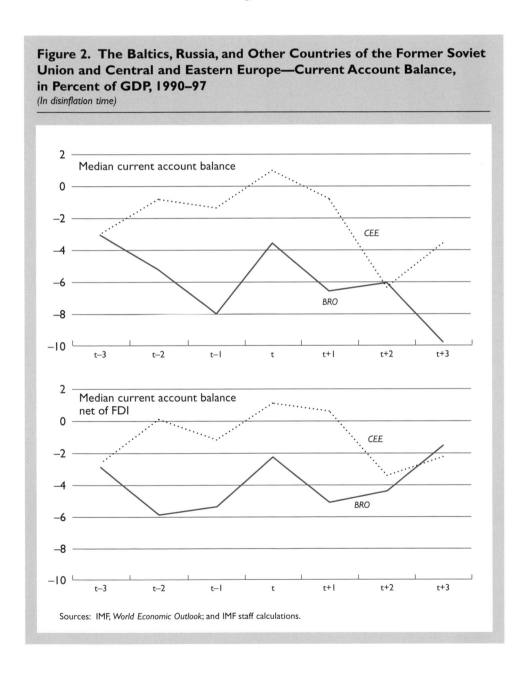

Sources: IMF, *World Economic Outlook*; and IMF staff calculations.

Disinflation and the External Current Account

Cukierman (1992) notes that one of the motives for inflation is the perceived risk that disinflation may pose for the external current account. An exchange rate based disinflation may lead to a real appreciation and, thus, affect competitiveness; and competitiveness may also deteriorate in the context of a floating exchange regime if the nominal exchange rate overshoots (Dornbusch, 1976). Indeed, concerns about the possible impact of tighter monetary policies on the external current account have been mentioned by some country authorities (for example, in Hungary) as one of the reasons why accelerating disinflation through a tighter exchange rate policy or the shift to a float was regarded as excessively risky (Surányi and Vincze, 1998).

External current account deficits relative to GDP have increased significantly during the 1990s in both the Central and Eastern European countries and the Baltics, Russia, and other countries of the former Soviet Union. In the early 1990s, the median balance in both was close to zero, while in 1997, it was a deficit in excess of 5 percent of GDP.

Recasting the current account data in inflation stabilization time highlights possible links between these trends and disinflation. The top panel of Figure 2 shows that inflation stabilization was accompanied by a weakening of the external accounts: the external balance declined sharply after disinflation in the Central and Eastern European countries, recovering somewhat in the third year. The Baltics, Russia, and other countries of the former Soviet Union exhibit a smoother decline, of similar magnitude.

Evidence of a widening of the external accounts, however, should not necessarily be taken as a proof that stabilization was accompanied by a shift to an unsustainable external position. As noted above, stabilization is a precondition for growth and a recovery of investment. In transition economies, such an acceleration of investment should be expected to be financed partially from abroad, through FDI and other long-term capital inflows. In turn, these inflows are likely to increase in stabilized macroeconomic conditions. Thus, the observed weakening of the external account after the stabilization may, at least in part, reflect the recovery of growth and investment, rather than an unsustainable loss of competitiveness. In this respect, it is useful to note that the external current account net of FDI in stabilization time shows stronger trends (bottom panel of Figure 2): the debt-financed external balance weakens markedly in the Central and Eastern European countries in the first two years, while in the Baltics, Russia, and other countries of the former Soviet Union, the initial weakening is less marked. But by the third year, the balance has strengthened considerably due to the strong inflow of FDI.

IV Inflation Inertia, Credibility, and Disinflation

The speed of disinflation and the apparent resilience of output in that context are remarkable features of transition economies' disinflation experience, and they are evident in the stabilizations of cases of extreme and more moderate inflation.

This section will suggest that disinflation reflected the implementation of decisive financial policies that curtailed excessive monetary growth, and that the absence of evidence of output costs in this context reflected various combinations of low inflation inertia and policy credibility.[8] In the highest inflation cases, inflation uncertainty was reflected in a shortening of the duration of nominal contracts, implying that aggregate price expectations were formed for relatively brief periods. This flexibility reduced output losses during decisive disinflation. In these cases, it was more important that financial policies were adjusted to eliminate the source of inflation than that they were adjusted credibly. But in the cases of less extreme inflation, where the duration of nominal contracts was largely unchanged, inflation inertia remained present. In these cases, policy credibility likely played a greater role in accounting for the low output costs associated with rapid disinflation.

The discussion attempts to identify the factors that facilitated the tightening of monetary policy needed to disinflate the economy, those that account for the evidence of limited output cost during inflation stabilization, and the extent to which these factors also explain the relatively slow disinflation in some countries, particularly during the poststabilization period. It addresses first the context in which disinflation occurred; second, the role played by fiscal policy; third, the role of credibility-enhancing devices; and last, the speed and sequencing of disinflation and structural reform. It concludes that fiscal consolidation and the decision of most authorities to disinflate rapidly were key to the success and the low output cost of these disinflations.

The Context for Disinflation

In many respects, the context for disinflation was more favorable than it might have appeared to be: inflation had not persisted for long; backward indexation was limited; the financial system, though fragile, turned out to be less susceptible to stress from disinflation than feared; and political economy factors favored disinflation in some countries. Furthermore, while price liberalization and relative price adjustment initially boosted the price level, they subsequently facilitated disinflation efforts.

Where these circumstances did not hold, disinflation was slower. For example, widespread indexation was a problem in Poland and Slovenia, two of the slow disinflation cases identified in Section II. In Hungary—another slow disinflater—creeping inflation had persisted throughout the 1980s, possibly contributing to the stickiness of inflation expectations lamented by policymakers in that country (Surányi and Vincze, 1998). Unresolved financial sector problems contributed to the inflation reversal in Albania and Bulgaria. And gradual administered price adjustments slowed down disinflation significantly in some countries (notably in Moldova and Ukraine).

Indexation

Backward indexation implies a lagged response of nominal wages to prices. This raises the output cost of disinflation, thereby reducing its credibility. Formal indexation, however, was exceptional in transition countries, possibly reflecting that while inflation had been violent, it had also been relatively brief, so that indexation had not had time to take root. As a result, even though wages and prices were frequently adjusted in the higher inflation cases,

---

[8]Policy credibility is a key factor in affecting the output cost of disinflation. If a disinflation package is credible, inflation expectations will decline rapidly, bringing down nominal interest rates and nominal wage growth. This will reduce the risk that disinflation is accompanied by an initial rise in real wages and real interest rates and the output losses associated with that. Of course, another factor at play is the duration of wage and lending contracts. If this duration is short, as it is likely when inflation is high, wage and interest rate dynamics can react more rapidly to changes in inflation.

only six countries out of the sample of 25 transition economies ever used backward-looking indexation.[9] And one of these (Croatia) abolished indexation at the start of the disinflation program. Even when indexation was present, it did not always increase inflation inertia. Where goods and factor prices were de facto indexed to the exchange rate, such as in Bulgaria, exchange rate stabilization fed directly into the stabilization of domestic prices.

The only two countries where indexation was pervasive are Poland and Slovenia. Both countries are part of the slow disinflation group, and there is evidence that indexation contributed to keeping these countries in the moderate inflation range for an extensive period (Pujol and Griffiths, 1998; and Ross, 1998).

Financial Fragility

The banking sector in all these economies was critically weak in the early stages of transition: two-tier systems and the associated legislative and accounting frameworks were generally in their infancy, and the banks were ill-prepared for a competitive environment, let alone one in which output, relative prices, and the price level were subject to major shocks.

While restructuring to address these problems would have facilitated disinflation by improving the strength, efficiency, and competitiveness of the financial system, it also seemed probable that disinflation would exacerbate financial fragility. This appeared likely to complicate disinflation efforts: the additional call on fiscal resources directly would challenge the fiscal consolidation; the additional calls on central bank refinance could undermine the monetary framework; the commitment to sustain disinflation might be weakened by concerns that increased interest rates could have indiscriminate effects, given poor credit assessment; and higher real interest rates could further undermine credit quality if solvent borrowers who expected to repay disproportionately stopped borrowing. Another potential danger, underscored by Cukierman (1992) with reference to nontransition economies, was that the monetary tightening associated with disinflation might be accompanied by lower bank interest rate spreads—owing to the longer maturity of lending rates than deposit rates.

Despite these difficulties, disinflations were rarely accompanied by up-front bank restructuring. In only

two cases—the former Yugoslav Republic of Macedonia and Slovenia—were operations to buttress the banking system initiated at the same time as disinflation, and even in these cases, the measures taken began, rather than completed, the task. Furthermore, despite the manifest weakness of many financial systems, rarely were these concerns uppermost in the authorities' minds when weighing the risks and modalities of disinflation.

There were several reasons why financial fragility did not undermine monetary control and the credibility of disinflation. In some of the high-inflation cases, the financial system had shrunk in real terms prior to disinflation due to negative real interest rates. For example, in Georgia and Moldova in 1994, M2 was 3 percent of GDP and 12 percent of GDP, respectively, and even now in the Baltics, Russia, and other countries of the former Soviet Union overall, banking system claims on nongovernment agencies are roughly half the level relative to GDP of Organization for Economic Cooperation and Development (OECD) countries. This contained the fiscal and refinancing contingent liabilities posed by financial fragility. Furthermore, while a number of banks had profited from transactions predicated on the high-inflation environment, this source of income was rarely critical to their overall profitability. So the demise of that environment rarely affected the overall health of individual banks, or of the banking system.

Fast disinflation and the maintenance of banking spreads also diminished the risk that financial fragility would deepen. The potential sluggishness of lending rates with respect to deposit rates when monetary policy is tightened turned out to be unimportant. At times, the contractual basis for bank loans was sufficiently unclear that lending rates were rapidly adjustable in practice, though more often, banks had shifted to variable rate or short-term lending prior to disinflation. Furthermore, nominal interest rates started falling rapidly along with inflation. So even to the limited extent that lending rates were stickier than deposit rates, rapidly falling inflation allowed spreads to widen during disinflation.

This is not to say that financial instability played no role, or that it may not become a problem in the future. Banking difficulties occurred during the Baltic and Czech disinflations. And most countries had to recapitalize banks at some point, though these operations were generally financed by issuing bonds, rather than by printing money, softening their impact on inflation. In addition, as illustrated by Estonia in 1993, firm decisions were taken to restructure or close banks, rather than to recapitalize them. But in addition to these direct links between financial fragility and inflation, indirect links also played a role. In the Czech Republic, a combination of banking inefficiencies, re-

---

[9]Those from the Baltics, Russia, and other countries of the former Soviet Union that continued the Soviet era practice of linking social payments to the minimum wage did not thereby establish de facto backward-looking indexation, as adjustments of the minimum wage were ad hoc in scale and timing.

flected in large interest rate spreads, accompanied by confidence in the currency, may have induced both domestic disintermediation and capital inflows in the mid-1990s. In this way, financial fragility may have indirectly stoked inflationary pressures.

While fragility remains, there are risks of further calls on the budget and for central bank refinance, and the financial sector's contribution to flexibility and performance of the whole economy is diminished. Albania and Bulgaria show that, even though much-abused financial systems can survive a remarkably long time, they eventually collapse with serious implications for macroeconomic stability. Recent difficulties in a medium-sized regional bank in Croatia underline that strong inflation performers are not immune from these difficulties. And the exchange rate crisis in Russia in August 1998 reflected to some extent increases in liquidity to sustain the banking sector. While progress has been made in strengthening financial structures and supervision in most transition countries, significant risks remain (see Appendix II).

Political Economy

Social and political characteristics of the preinflation stabilization period may also account for the decisiveness of the disinflation effort and its credibility. In some Central and Eastern European countries and in the Baltic States, the perceived short-term costs of disinflation were seen as the price of national liberation. This muted the political backlash to "shock therapies," and partly explains why determined reformers were often politically successful (Åslund, Boone, and Johnson, 1996). Moreover, when the old economic interest groups were discredited and disorganized, an opening for "extraordinary politics"—in the words of Poland's Finance Minister Balcerowicz (Bruno, 1996)—appeared, which eased the introduction of tough disinflation and reform programs, albeit sometimes only temporarily.

Such openings were, however, rarely apparent in most BRO countries (outside the Baltics), which partly explains why disinflation was often delayed there. Even in some Central and Eastern European countries, such as Bulgaria and Romania, it proved impossible to gather sufficient political support to implement sustained disinflation. In some cases, coalitions of various political interests may have delayed disinflation. Bruno (1996) notes that a high-inflation equilibrium can be generated when interest groups disagree on who should bear the brunt of the adjustment. In other cases, interest groups may have had an indirect interest in inflation, having privileged access to fiscal subsidies or transfers that generate it. Clearly, political instability and war played a key role in delaying disinflation in Armenia, Croatia, Georgia, and Tajikistan. Disagreement between the central bank and the government on the appropriate policy course or insufficient understanding of the economics of inflation—the view that inflation was caused by "speculators" rather than by financial policies—were also factors in some countries (notably, Belarus, Bulgaria, Tajikistan, Turkmenistan, Uzbekistan, and, initially, Ukraine).

By the mid-1990s, however, even in cases where political impediments to disinflation had been most severe, it had become apparent to most policymakers that inflation was a monetary phenomenon fueled by large fiscal and quasi-fiscal deficits. At the same time, the costs of inflation for vulnerable social groups (such as pensioners) were becoming apparent.[10] These factors may have eventually strengthened the resolve to stabilize and the credibility of the disinflation programs subsequently implemented.

Relative Price Disequilibria

The environment for disinflation was complicated by the need for large relative price changes, given that relative prices were far from competitive equilibrium, combined in some cases with monopolistic pricing that emerged after price liberalization (IMF, 1997, pp. 108–11). A shock in relative prices, from either source, risks inducing inflation if there is downward price stickiness. If this pressure is accommodated to avoid an output loss, inflation will rise, with legal or de facto indexation delaying the disinflation process.

In transition economies, the inflationary pressure arising from relative price changes was exacerbated by the type of price shocks that accompanied the transition. Prior to the transition, some goods were largely underpriced while most were marginally overpriced (Pujol and Griffiths, 1998; and Coorey, Mecagni, and Offerdal, 1998). This pattern imparted an inflationary impulse because, while the few largely underpriced goods were rapidly repriced, the many overpriced goods were not cut (possibly reflecting microeconomic adjustment costs) and so were adjusted in real terms through inflation (Ball and Mankiw, 1994).

The role of relative price adjustments in inflation was particularly strong in the early phases of the transition when most prices were liberalized, but seems to have declined over time (Pujol and Griffiths, 1998; Coorey, Mecagni, and Offerdal, 1998; Cottarelli, Griffiths, and Moghadam, 1998; Kra-

---

[10]Bulir (1998) finds evidence from a large sample of developing countries that high inflation increases economic inequality. Evidence on the drop in real pensions and its relation with inflation in 11 transition economies can be found in Cangiano, Cottarelli, and Cubeddu (1998). Other aspects of inequality in transition are discussed in EBRD (1997).

Box 1. Relative Prices and Inflation: A Look Ahead

Several years into the transition, goods price levels and structures remain distinct from industrial countries (Koen and De Masi, 1997). This does not necessarily mean, however, that a rapid convergence should be expected, as price levels and structures are generally correlated with GDP (Nuxoll, 1996). Market-determined prices are likely to converge to industrial country standards only in the long run. Thus, the main contribution of relative price changes to inflation in the near future is likely to come primarily from changes in administered prices.

The remaining inflationary potential from changes in administered prices depends on the share of administered prices in the CPI, how far they are below their market-determined level, and the response of other prices. In most cases, the share of administered prices in the baskets used to calculate the CPI is small, albeit possibly understated to the extent that the weights have not been fully adjusted as administered prices have been raised toward full cost coverage (Table 3). In only a few cases is removing all remaining price controls thought likely to add more than 10 percentage points to the CPI (Table 3).[1] But in some low-inflation countries

(such as the Czech Republic and Croatia), as well as in some moderate high-inflation countries (Belarus), administered price increases could put significant pressure on inflation developments.

The reaction of nonadministered prices to changes in administered prices will depend, inter alia, on the degree of indexation, the overall credibility of the authorities, and, of course, the degree of monetary accommodation. In countries where the authorities' credibility is in doubt, an increase in administered prices may be regarded as signaling that inflation is accelerating, and lead to parallel increases in all prices. A case in point is Romania where in early 1997, the increase in some energy prices started a wave of general price increases. Conversely, the recent experience in Azerbaijan shows that even fairly large increases in administered prices can be absorbed with only a temporary rise in inflation.

Finally, there is evidence that after the initial impact of relative price changes on inflation, price liberalization is generally found to reduce inflation (Fischer, Sahay, and Végh, 1996; and Cottarelli, Griffiths, and Moghadam, 1998). This may be due to the fact that those countries that adjusted to administered prices more slowly through subsidies or price controls, such as Moldova, experienced larger fiscal or quasi-fiscal deficits, and due to the boost to supply-side flexibility that price liberalization engenders.

---

[1]These estimates neither take into account the reaction of other prices nor the degree of monetary accommodation. Moreover, the figures should be taken cum grano salis as, in many cases, it is difficult to evaluate what the market-determined price of certain products would be. Comparisons with industrial countries may be misleading for products (as services) that involve significant labor input. The case of rents is also complex: Zavoico (1995) argues that rents in transition countries may not

need to incorporate amortization costs for a number of years, because currently there is an excess supply of houses.

---

jnyák and Klingen, 1998; and Woźniak, 1998). This is because the relative price adjustment process appears to have been fairly rapid, partly reflecting limited indexation in most countries (Koen and De Masi, 1997). A key remaining inflationary impulse from relative price changes concerns administrative price adjustments.[11] However, with price ceilings applied only to a limited number of products (energy, transportation, rents, and utilities), these have also declined in importance (Box 1).

Policy Response: Fiscal Policy

The early phase of the transition was accompanied by large fiscal imbalances in virtually all transition

countries, as a result of falling revenues and rigid public expenditure. Government securities markets were virtually nonexistent and access to foreign finance was limited. So the emerging deficits had to be monetized when the potential for direct funding from the banking sector was exhausted. Of the Baltics, Russia, and other countries of the former Soviet Union, seven of 15 countries recorded seignorage in excess of 10 percent of GDP in 1993, when inflation was at or near its peak (Ghosh, 1997).

The development of a broader range of financing options for government alongside fiscal consolidation were key elements underlying the subsequent disinflations. The former reduced the pressure for monetization, given public deficits,[12] and the latter reduced the risk of explosive paths for public debt-to-GDP ratios (Buiter, 1997). This reduced inflationary pressures arising from the expectation of future monetization (Sargent and Wallace, 1981).

---

[11]In Belarus and Ukraine, administered price adjustments spurred inflation, as did energy and other price increases in Romania alongside liberalization of the exchange rate in early 1997. Administrative price changes were most important in Hungary in the early 1990s, and again in 1995–96, when increased energy prices stimulated a renewed acceleration of inflation.

[12]In some cases, however, the additional financing option provided by new securities may have facilitated increased fiscal deficits. Ukraine through 1997 may be one example of this.

Table 3. Administered Price Changes

| | Weight of Administered Price Changes on CPI | Estimated Effect on the CPI of Removing Administered Price Controls | | Inflation Rate End-1997 |
		Minimum	Maximum	
Albania	5	2	3	42.1
Bulgaria	15	6	12	578.6
Croatia	18	4	10	4.4
Czech Republic	15–20	5	6	10.0
Hungary	15	2	4	18.4
Macedonia, FYR	30	2	3	2.7
Poland	11	3	6	13.2
Romania	13	2	5	151.6
Slovak Republic	15–20	5	6	6.5
Slovenia	28	3	9	9.5
Armenia	...	...	...	22.0
Azerbaijan	30	1	2	0.4
Belarus	33	15	25	63.4
Estonia	22	...	...	12.5
Georgia	...	...	...	7.2
Kazakhstan	10	1	2	11.3
Kyrgyz Republic	10	5	10	14.7
Latvia	20	5	10	7.0
Lithuania	17	1	3	8.5
Moldova	15	2	5	11.1
Russia	7	4	7	11.0
Tajikistan	7–8	15	20	163.1
Turkmenistan	3	...	...	21.8
Ukraine	16	3	5	10.1
Uzbekistan	8[1]	...	...	50.0

Source: IMF staff estimates.

[1]Includes energy and utility prices only. If the prices of basic consumer goods—including flour, sugar, bread, and so on—are also included, the weight of administered prices is at least 40 percent.

Government Securities Markets

By 1997, all transition economies (with the exception of Estonia, Tajikistan, and the former Yugoslav Republic of Macedonia) had introduced primary treasury bill markets—mostly based on auctions—with many of the Baltics, Russia, and other countries of the former Soviet Union joining the group in 1995–96 (Table 4). In the most advanced transition economies (such as the Czech Republic, Hungary, and Poland), primary government securities markets are more fully developed, and secondary markets are also active, usually organized around a system of primary dealers. The Baltics, Russia, and other countries of the former Soviet Union are lagging behind. However, "moderate" or "substantial" progress had been achieved by 1997 in most of the Baltics, Russia, and other countries of the former Soviet Union (IMF, 1997).[13] As a

result, the share of fiscal deficits financed by issuing domestic government securities is now sizable in a number of transition economies (Table 4).

Fiscal Consolidation

Public finances strengthened significantly during 1993–97. The average fiscal deficit-to-GDP ratio fell from 13½ percent in 1992 to 3½ percent in 1997; the decline was faster in the Baltics, Russia, and other countries of the former Soviet Union, but it was sizable also in Central and Eastern European countries (Table 5). Quasi-fiscal deficits—whose importance for macroeconomic developments has been stressed

---

[13]Qualitative assessments provided by IMF desk economists, summarized in index form (see Cottarelli, Griffiths, and Moghadam, 1998) also indicate significant progress in developing

financial markets: on a 1–10 scale (10 indicating the degree of development of government securities markets in industrial countries), the index for the Baltics, Russia, and other countries of the former Soviet Union improved from 2.1 in 1993 to 5.5 in 1996, while that for Central and Eastern European countries improved from 4.4 to 5.6. As this index reflects subjective assessments, it should be taken as indicative of the direction of change, rather than for cross-country comparisons.

Table 4. Development of Government Securities Markets

	Date of Introduction of Treasury Bills	Share of General Government Deficit Covered by Sales of Securities, Excluding Sales to Domestic Banks (1997)	Degree of Development of Interbank and Government Securities Markets (1997)
Albania	1994	—	—
Bulgaria	1993	26.4	—
Croatia	1996	21.7	—
Czech Republic	1991	75.0	Substantial
Hungary	Before 1990	30.1	Substantial
Macedonia, FYR	No treasury bill market	0.0	Substantial
Poland	1991	70.4	—
Romania	1997	9.6	Limited
Slovak Republic	1991	—	Substantial
Slovenia	1990	9.0	—
Armenia	1995	8.8	Limited
Azerbaijan	1996	—	Limited
Belarus	1994	21.5	Limited
Estonia	No treasury bill market	—	Moderate
Georgia	1997	0.1	Moderate
Kazakhstan	1994	2.3	Substantial
Kyrgyz Republic	1996	3.3	Moderate
Latvia	1993	25.9	Substantial
Lithuania	1994	−29.6	Moderate
Moldova	1995	11.0	Moderate
Russia	1993	39.5	Substantial
Tajikistan	No treasury bill market	—	Limited
Turkmenistan	1994	—	Limited
Ukraine	1996	50.6	Moderate
Uzbekistan	1996	8.9	Limited

Source: IMF staff estimates.

several times (Mackenzie and Stella, 1996; and Buiter, 1997)—also abated (see below).

A simple plot of inflation against the overall and primary fiscal balances of transition economies suggests that fiscal consolidation was closely related to the decline in inflation during 1993–97 (Figure 3).[14] A closer look at individual country data (Tables 6 and 7) reveals five key features: (1) a sizable fiscal tightening—with a corresponding tightening of money creation through credit to the government—characterized most inflation stabilization cases, a key finding of earlier reviews of the transition experience (Bruno, 1992); (2) fiscal adjustment focused on expenditure cuts; (3) when fiscal adjustment did not accompany the inflation stabilization, the fiscal position was already strong; (4) inflation stabilization did not require a fiscal position that was solvent according to standard formulas; and (5) the link between fiscal tightening and disinflation is weaker in moderate inflation cases.

Fiscal adjustment (typically up-front fiscal adjustment in the disinflation year or the year before) accompanied the drop in inflation in 13 of the 20 inflation stabilization cases observed during 1993–97 (Table 6). In two additional cases—Bulgaria (second disinflation) and Lithuania—the primary balance changed little, but quasi-fiscal losses were substantially reduced. In Lithuania, losses accruing as a result of arbitrage of interrepublican accounts after withdrawal from the ruble area were curtailed. In Bulgaria, quasi-fiscal losses accruing in both the financial and nonfinancial enterprise sectors as a result of widespread soft budget constraints were reduced under the first stabilization, albeit only to reemerge later, inducing a reversal of the associated disinflation gains. Quasi-fiscal deficits—particularly in the form of directed credit—were reduced also in countries that cut the general government deficits, especially in the Baltics, Russia, and other countries of the former Soviet Union (a case in point is Kazakhstan).

---

[14]Focusing on the relationship between inflation and primary balance is important as the latter is not affected by the fall in interest expenditure that accompanies disinflation. This fall makes it more difficult to interpret the causal link between decline in the overall deficit and decline in inflation (see footnote 1 in Box 2).

Table 5. Overall and Primary General Government Balances, and Central Bank Financing to the Government[1]
(In percent of GDP)

	Overall Balance							Primary Balance[2]							Central Bank Financing					
	1991	1992	1993	1994	1995	1996	1997	1991	1992	1993	1994	1995	1996	1997	1992	1993	1994	1995	1996	1997
Albania	...	-21.8	-15.4	-13.0	-10.4	-12.6	-13.1	...	-20.6	-13.0	-10.6	-8.2	-9.3	-7.4	20.0	9.1	6.6	2.0	1.0	6.0
Bulgaria	-14.6	-5.2	-10.9	-5.8	-6.3	-12.7	-2.5	-14.6	1.2	-1.6	7.7	7.9	6.3	6.0	6.0	11.0	5.5	4.9	14.5	-0.1
Croatia	-5.1	-3.9	-0.8	1.6	-0.9	-0.4	-1.3	-4.9	-4.6	2.1	1.9	-1.1	0.7	0.2	...	...	-0.7	0.5	-0.1	0.0
Czech Republic	...	-2.1	0.5	-1.2	-1.8	-1.2	-2.1	...	...	...	-0.1	-1.1	-0.4	-0.9	...	-2.1	-2.4	-1.0	-0.8	0.7
Hungary	-3.7	-6.9	-8.4	-8.2	-6.2	-3.1	-4.8	2.1	-1.7	-4.0	-2.8	2.7	4.0	3.5	16.5	13.2	11.2	7.5	7.3	1.7
Macedonia, FYR	...	-9.8	-13.4	-2.9	-1.2	-0.5	-0.4	...	...	-9.7	-0.2	0.5	1.8	1.0	...	...	1.3	0.1	0.1	0.4
Poland	-6.7	-6.2	-3.4	-3.2	-3.3	-3.6	-3.3	...	-10.9	-1.3	1.2	1.0	0.1	1.2	5.2	1.5	1.5	0.1	0.1	0.5
Romania	3.3	-4.6	-0.4	-1.9	-2.6	-4.0	-3.6	3.3	-4.4	0.6	-0.5	-1.3	-2.6	-0.2	...	...	...	...	...	...
Slovak Republic	...	-11.9	-7.0	-1.3	0.2	-1.3	-5.1	...	-10.9	-4.0	2.5	2.4	0.9	-3.0	...	...	...	...	...	1.5
Slovenia	...	0.2	0.3	-0.2	0.0	0.3	-1.1	...	0.2	0.5	0.5	0.2	-0.3	-2.6	0.0	0.0	0.0	0.0	0.0	0.0
Armenia[3]	-1.9	...	-54.3	-10.1	-12.0	-9.3	-5.9	...	...	...	-8.2	-8.0	-6.7	-4.1	...	...	3.5	0.4	1.4	-1.4
Azerbaijan	-5.0	-29.0	-15.4	-12.1	-4.9	-2.8	-1.7	...	...	...	-11.4	-4.1	-2.4	-1.2	0.0	11.4	8.2	-2.7	1.4	-0.6
Belarus	1.9	0.0	-1.9	-2.5	-1.9	-1.6	-0.7	...	0.7	-1.0	-2.1	-1.1	-0.9	-0.7	...	...	0.8	2.6	1.4	0.4
Estonia	5.2	-0.3	-0.6	1.3	-1.2	-1.5	2.0	...	...	-0.4	1.3	-0.9	-1.3	2.3	...	0.0	0.0	0.0	0.0	0.0
Georgia	-3.1	-62.3	-26.1	-16.5	-4.5	-4.4	-3.8	...	-62.3	-26.0	-14.1	-3.1	-3.4	-2.4	...	...	2.0	1.8	2.7	2.2
Kazakhstan	-8.8	-7.3	-4.1	-7.7	-3.2	-5.3	-7.0	...	-7.3	-10.2	-10.7	-9.3	-12.7	-2.9	...	...	3.2	1.7	-0.1	-0.3
Kyrgyz Republic	3.9	-14.8	-14.4	-11.6	-17.3	-9.5	-9.4	...	...	-13.8	-11.4	-16.9	-8.4	-7.7	...	0.7	1.3	7.8	1.9	0.4
Latvia	6.3	0.5	-5.3	-4.8	-4.5	-1.4	-1.8	...	-0.7	1.6	-1.4	-2.1	-0.2	2.2	0.0	0.0	0.0	0.0	0.0	0.0
Lithuania[4]	0.0	-0.8	0.6	-4.1	-3.3	-1.4	1.3	...	...	-5.9	-5.9	-4.6	-4.2	-0.5	0.0	0.0	0.0	0.0	0.0	0.0
Moldova	0.0	-23.9	-7.4	-9.1	-5.8	-6.6	-6.8	...	-23.9	-6.3	-6.2	-2.3	-4.0	-3.1	26.1	5.0	1.9	1.5	-0.7	1.4
Russia	-14.9	-6.6	-8.6	-10.5	-7.9	-9.5	-7.9	...	-17.1	-6.1	-8.4	-3.6	-2.5	-3.1	9.2	5.9	8.1	1.6	2.1	1.5
Tajikistan	-15.9	-30.5	-23.4	-5.1	-11.2	-5.8	-3.7	...	...	...	...	-8.4	-4.6	-2.1	30.6	24.8	9.6	13.1	2.3	1.5
Turkmenistan	2.4	13.3	-0.5	-1.4	-1.6	0.3	0.0	...	...	...	-1.2	-1.0	-1.2	-0.2	9.9	6.0	1.6	1.8	-0.2	0.4
Ukraine	-13.6	-23.2	-9.7	-8.7	-4.9	-3.2	-5.6	...	-23.2	-9.5	-9.5	-3.5	-2.1	-3.2	23.8	14.1	8.9	5.6	2.1	1.4
Uzbekistan	...	-18.5	-10.4	-6.1	-4.1	-7.3	-2.8	...	-11.9	-18.3	-1.0	-3.5	-5.7	-2.3	...	...	4.8	1.4	6.8	1.3

Source: IMF staff estimates.

[1]For the countries that stabilized during 1993–97, shaded areas indicate periods in which inflation dropped below the stabilization threshold (see definition in Table 2).

[2]The primary balance is calculated as the general government balance minus net interest payments. Primary balance calculations exclude interest receipts for Armenia, Azerbaijan, Belarus, Estonia, Kazakhstan, Kyrgyz Republic, Romania, Slovakia, and the Ukraine.

[3]The higher overall deficit in 1995, the first stabilization year, is due to the payment of arrears related to government-guaranteed domestic loans.

[4]About one-half of the deficit in Lithuania during 1993–96 was due to net lending.

Figure 3. Transition Economies: Fiscal Performance Versus Inflation Performance, 1994–97
(In percent)

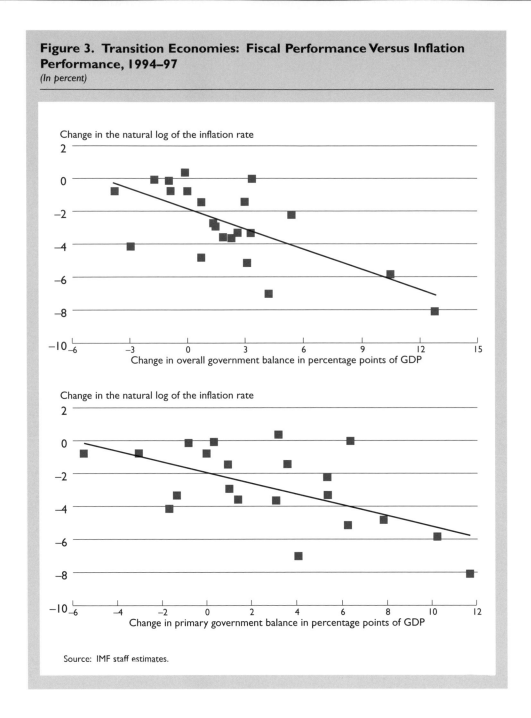

Source: IMF staff estimates.

Fiscal consolidation allowed a sharp contraction in central bank credit to the government. In the 20 inflation stabilization cases, the average flow of central bank credit to the government fell from 10.6 percent of GDP in 1992 to 0.7 percent of GDP in 1997 (Table 5), contributing significantly to the decline in the growth rate of money (see below).

In almost all the above cases, the adjustment consisted primarily of expenditure cuts. Only in Croatia, Latvia, and Uzbekistan did the revenue-to-GDP ratio

rise significantly, and only temporarily in the latter case. In the former Yugoslav Republic of Macedonia, after an initial increase in the revenue ratio, both expenditure and revenue ratios started declining. In six countries (Armenia, Azerbaijan, Belarus, the Kyrgyz Republic, Russia, and Ukraine), revenue ratios declined during disinflation. The predominance of expenditure rather than revenue adjustment to close fiscal imbalances may have helped the disinflation directly, given that tax increases often pro-

Table 6. Fiscal and Inflation Developments

	Stabilization Quarter[1]	Fiscal Developments
		(Stabilization cases)
Albania	1993: Q1	Up-front adjustment based on expenditure cuts
Armenia	1995: Q2	Up-front adjustment, further progress later; cuts in expenditures and revenues
Azerbaijan	1995: Q2	Up-front adjustment, further progress later; cuts in expenditures and revenues
Belarus	1995: Q4	Up-front adjustment, cuts in expenditure and decline in revenue
Bulgaria (1st stabilization)	1995: Q1	Modest up-front adjustment, based on cuts in expenditures and revenues
Bulgaria (2nd stabilization)	1997: Q2	Strong primary surplus maintained; cuts in expenditures and revenues
Croatia	1994: Q1	Up-front adjustment based on revenue increases
Estonia	1993: Q4	Small primary surplus
Georgia	1994: Q4	Up-front adjustment, based on expenditure cuts
Kazakhstan	1995: Q2	Up-front adjustment based on expenditure cuts and reduction in quasi-fiscal deficits
Kyrgyz Republic	1995: Q2	Adjustment in 1994, with a temporary reversal in 1995; adjustment based on expenditure cuts
Latvia	1993: Q1	Small primary surplus
Lithuania	1994: Q1	Constant fairly sizable primary deficit, but strong reduction in quasi-fiscal deficit
Macedonia, FYR	1994: Q2	Up-front adjustment, with initial increases in revenues and expenditure cuts, followed by cuts in both revenues and expenditures
Moldova	1994: Q2	Up-front adjustment based on expenditure cuts
Romania	1994: Q3	Fiscal weakening and sizable quasi-fiscal deficits
Russia	1995: Q4	Up-front adjustment in the primary balance, followed by a partial relaxation; cuts in expenditure and revenues
Turkmenistan	1997: Q2	Small primary deficit maintained
Ukraine	1997: Q2	Up-front adjustment based on expenditure cuts, in cash terms. New arrears offset the expenditure reductions
Uzbekistan	1995: Q2	Up-front adjustment based on revenue increases
		(Countries that maintained inflation at moderate levels)
Hungary	—	Strong fiscal consolidation
Poland	—	Fiscal improvement
		(Low inflation countries)
Czech Republic	—	Declining primary surplus, with unchanged overall balance
Slovak Republic	—	Stable primary surplus
Slovenia	—	Stable primary surplus
		(Countries that failed to stabilize)
Tajikistan	—	Strong fiscal improvement

Source: IMF staff estimates.

[1]Quarter in which the 60 percent inflation threshold was broken (see Table 2).

duce a one-off increase in the price level, particularly indirect taxes (Surányi and Vincze, 1998).

There are cases where fiscal strengthening did not accompany inflation stabilization. In Estonia, Latvia, and Turkmenistan, the fiscal position prior to stabilization was already fairly strong, and other factors underlay persistent inflation in that context. In Estonia, inflation was driven by price developments in Russia before June 1992, when an independent currency issued under a currency board was introduced. Thereafter, inflation fell sharply, but as Latvia also experienced later, the exchange rate peg was insufficient to eliminate inflation, despite the firm fiscal stance. In Turkmenistan, the reasons for the persistence of inflation are more difficult to assess, although they may have been related to the increasing scarcity of imported consumer goods until early 1997, when the central bank was allowed to sell foreign exchange on the market, relieving the shortage. In contrast to these cases, inflation in Tajikistan persisted in spite of the significant strengthening of the primary balance during 1996–98 because of political instability and civil war.

Table 7. General Government Revenue and Primary Expenditures in Transition Economies[1]

(In percent of GDP)

	General Government Revenue							Primary Expenditure[2]						
	1991	1992	1993	1994	1995	1996	1997	1991	1992	1993	1994	1995	1996	1997
Albania	...	22.5	24.9	23.3	23.9	19.0	17.2	...	43.1	37.9	34.0	32.1	28.3	24.7
Bulgaria	40.4	38.4	37.2	39.9	36.1	32.5	31.1	54.9	37.1	38.8	32.3	28.1	26.2	25.4
Croatia	216.9	32.2	34.2	42.2	44.1	45.4	45.0	39.9	36.8	32.1	40.3	45.2	44.7	44.2
Czech Republic	59.1	45.0	45.9	44.7	43.5	42.5	40.7	...	...	...	44.8	44.6	42.8	41.7
Hungary	53.5	53.1	53.7	51.2	47.6	46.5	45.7	51.4	54.8	57.7	54.0	44.9	42.5	41.3
Macedonia, FYR	8.2	39.3	40.2	46.4	42.0	41.0	38.9	...	...	49.9	46.6	41.5	39.2	36.9
Poland	42.3	43.3	47.1	46.0	44.8	44.0	44.5	49.3	54.2	48.4	44.8	43.8	43.9	43.6
Romania	41.9	37.4	33.9	32.1	31.9	29.8	27.7	38.6	41.7	33.3	32.6	33.2	32.4	29.7
Slovak Republic	50.7	46.0	44.2	46.4	46.9	47.4	40.9	...	57.0	48.2	44.0	44.5	46.5	44.0
Slovenia	0.6	45.8	47.0	45.9	45.7	45.2	43.8	...	45.6	46.6	45.4	45.5	45.5	47.3
Armenia	27.6	29.1	28.9	27.7	19.9	17.7	19.8	...	...	...	35.9	27.9	24.4	22.6
Azerbaijan	...	...	33.5	24.5	15.3	16.2	18.2	...	...	...	35.9	19.4	18.6	19.4
Belarus	...	46.0	54.3	47.5	42.7	40.9	46.1	...	45.3	55.3	49.6	43.8	41.9	46.8
Estonia	...	...	38.6	41.1	39.9	39.0	38.9	...	...	39.0	39.8	40.8	40.3	36.7
Georgia	34.1	13.1	12.4	7.7	7.1	9.4	10.2	...	75.5	38.4	21.8	10.1	12.8	12.5
Kazakhstan	27.6	24.5	21.1	18.5	16.9	13.2	13.3	36.5	31.7	31.3	29.2	26.2	25.9	26.3
Kyrgyz Republic	...	...	24.7	20.8	16.7	15.9	17.0	...	...	38.4	32.2	33.6	24.3	24.6
Latvia	37.4	28.1	36.4	36.5	35.5	36.7	39.4	31.1	28.8	34.8	37.9	37.6	36.9	37.6
Lithuania	...	...	30.2	31.7	32.3	29.6	32.7	...	...	36.1	37.6	36.9	33.7	34.4
Moldova	...	30.3	22.1	33.5	33.9	32.1	34.3	...	54.2	28.4	39.7	36.2	36.1	37.4
Russia	33.4	39.5	35.5	34.7	30.7	31.0	31.7	...	56.5	41.6	43.1	34.3	33.5	36.0
Tajikistan	...	...	...	...	15.2	12.1	11.7	...	...	...	...	23.6	16.7	15.8
Turkmenistan	38.2	42.2	22.6	10.4	12.5	15.4	29.2	...	...	...	11.6	13.5	16.6	28.9
Ukraine	...	34.2	42.8	41.9	37.8	36.7	38.4	...	57.4	52.3	51.3	41.3	38.8	40.2
Uzbekistan	...	31.5	35.3	32.3	34.6	34.2	30.2	...	43.4	53.6	33.3	38.1	39.9	33.0

Source: IMF staff estimates.

[1]For the countries that stabilized during 1993–97, shaded areas indicate years in which inflation was below the stabilization threshold (as defined in Table 2).

[2]The primary expenditure is calculated as the general government expenditure minus net interest payments. Primary balance calculations exclude interest receipts for Armenia, Azerbaijan, Belarus, Estonia, Kazakhstan, Kyrgyz Republic, Romania, Slovakia, and the Ukraine.

Box 2. Inflation and Fiscal Deficits: Summary of Econometric Results

The relationship between inflation and fiscal deficits in transition economies has been explored through regression analysis in several papers (Fischer, Sahay, and Végh, 1996; Lougani and Sheets, 1997; and Cottarelli, Griffiths, and Moghadam, 1998). All these papers find a significant statistical relationship between inflation and the fiscal deficit, which is robust to differences in the econometric specification and in the definition of the deficit.[1] Moreover, these studies show that fiscal factors remain important even after controlling for other factors (such as the exchange regime, measures of the overall progress in reforming the economy, central bank independence, indexation, and relative price changes).

The estimate of the direct quantitative effect of fiscal deficits on inflation is, however, relatively low. In most of the specifications, a decline in the deficit-to-GDP ratio of 1 percentage point when inflation is, say, 100 percent involves a decline in inflation of only 5–8 percentage points. The effect is larger at high inflation levels, but smaller when inflation is low.[2]

This result may be explained in two ways. First, in a number of countries, disinflation did not require a reduction in the deficit either because the fiscal position was already sufficiently strong or because the main problem was related to quasi-fiscal deficits. As the regression results "average out" the experience of all countries during the sample period, the effect of deficit cuts estimated from regressions using changes in the variables (rather than levels) appears to be lower than in reality for those countries that had a fiscal problem. Second, the results indicate that fiscal adjustment should not be seen in isolation but rather as a component of a comprehensive package that enhances the credibility of disinflation through appropriate exchange rate policies, and other institutional devices (such as central bank independence). One element of a comprehensive package may be the development of government securities markets. Cottarelli, Griffiths, and Moghadam (1998) report that the relation between inflation and fiscal deficits is stronger in those countries without a developed government securities market, presumably reflecting the greater reliance of such countries on central bank finance for the government deficit.

---

[1]In particular, Cottarelli, Griffiths, and Moghadam (1998) find that the relationship holds also after removing the effect of inflation on government interest payments, thus suggesting a line of causality that runs from fiscal deficits to inflation, and not vice versa.

[2]This is due to the semilogarithmic specification of the relation between inflation and fiscal deficits, adopted in all papers.

This specification seems to fit the data better than alternative specifications.

The only cases in which inflation stabilization succeeded while fiscal and quasi-fiscal deficits remained high were Romania and the Kyrgyz Republic. In the former case, the progress on inflation was ultimately reversed. In the latter case, there was a sharp temporary fiscal relaxation in 1995 associated with an election. But the inflationary impact of the fiscal position, both before and after this, was considerably less than is implied by the overall and primary fiscal balances. These reflect a large, import-intensive, and externally financed public investment program. Apart from 1995, domestic funding of the deficit remained about or below 2½ percent of GDP throughout the disinflation, and this shifted progressively from central bank to other sources of domestic finance. Thus, as with other cases, the Kyrgyz disinflation was underwritten by a firm fiscal position.

It is notable that inflation stabilization did not require fiscal solvency according to simple standard formulas. Such formulas identify the minimal primary balance necessary to avoid an explosive path for the debt-to-GDP ratio in terms of the initial debt level, the GDP growth rate, and the interest rate on debt (see formula in Table 8). By these standards, the fiscal position during most of the inflation stabilizations was insolvent, and still remained so in 1997.[15] The simple assumptions that underlie the formulas, however, may be particularly inappropriate in transition economies. Transition economies have strong potential productivity growth and this is likely to contribute to future strengthened primary balances. In addition, some of these countries also implemented structural reforms that bolstered long-term fiscal sustainability, even if they had little immediate fiscal impact.[16] This, and the fact that the Baltics and other countries of the former Soviet Union (excluding Russia) started the transition with negligible public debt and so could derive efficiency gains

---

[15]The table uses an interest rate-growth rate differential of 2 percentage points, as in the studies on transition economies by Budina and van Wijnbergen (1997) and Begg (1998).

[16]For example, the pension reforms approved in 1996 in Kazakhstan reduced future public liabilities without greatly affecting the current fiscal balance, and the reduction in arrears by the pension fund in the following year caused a deterioration in the measured fiscal balance.

Table 8. Actual and Sustainable Primary Fiscal Balances

(In percent of GDP)

	1997 Actual	Sustainable[1]
Albania	−7.4	1.1
Bulgaria	6.0	2.1
Croatia	0.2	0.6
Czech Republic	−0.9	0.2
Hungary	3.5	1.3
Macedonia, FYR	1.0	0.8
Poland	1.2	0.9
Romania	−0.2	0.4
Slovak Republic	−3.0	0.5
Slovenia	−2.6	0.4
Armenia	−4.1	0.8
Azerbaijan	−1.2	0.3
Belarus	−0.7	0.2
Estonia	2.3	0.1
Georgia	−2.4	0.6
Kazakhstan	−2.9	0.3
Kyrgyz Republic	−7.7	0.8
Latvia	2.2	0.3
Lithuania	−0.5	0.2
Moldova	−3.1	0.8
Russia	−3.1	0.4
Tajikistan	−2.5	1.6
Turkmenistan	−0.2	0.6
Ukraine	−3.2	0.4
Uzbekistan	−2.3	0.3

Source: IMF staff calculations.

[1]The sustainable primary balance is the primary balance that would allow stabilizing of the public debt-to-GDP ratio; it can be computed as

$$p = [(i-g)/(1+g)]d$$

where p is the primary balance-to-GDP ratio, i is the nominal interest rate on government debt, g is the nominal GDP growth rate, and d is the initial debt-to-GDP ratio. The figures in Table 8 have been based on a nominal GDP growth rate of 8 percent, and an interest rate-growth differential of 2 percentage points. Actual figures for end-1996 have been used for the debt-to-GDP ratio. It should be stressed that for countries with high debt/GDP ratios, stabilizing the debt-to-GDP ratio is unlikely to be sufficient to ensure long-run sustainability. Reducing vulnerability would require lowering the debt ratio and, therefore, stronger fiscal positions than indicated above.

from added leverage, may explain why strict adherence to the standard formulas has not been necessary to support or sustain disinflation.[17]

The link between disinflation and fiscal adjustment is less clear at moderate inflation levels, however. In the Czech Republic, inflation remained moderate de-

spite declining primary surpluses during 1993–96. Conversely, the drop in inflation in Slovenia during 1993–97, in the Slovak Republic during 1994–96, and in Poland during 1993–97 was not accompanied by a fiscal strengthening. Various factors may account for this. Moderate inflation countries are also relatively fast reformers with more developed government securities markets. This alleviates the monetary impact of fiscal deficits as illustrated by the case of Hungary, where large deficits in 1993–94 led to only a limited rise in inflation. In addition, once fiscal sustainability is achieved, disinflation may become a problem of expectation coordination (Blanchard, 1998). In this environment, a fiscal expansion that casts doubts on fiscal sustainability or that leads to overheating should be avoided, but a fiscal tightening may not be necessary. The results of more formal research into the relationship between fiscal balances, government securities markets, and inflation, at different inflation levels, are outlined in Box 2.

These findings have implications for fiscal policy in sustaining the progress toward low inflation. Fiscal consolidation, having been so central to laying the groundwork for inflation stabilization, will remain essential to sustain disinflation. Those countries that already have a strong underlying fiscal position, implying that inflation is an expectational problem, should maintain this strong fiscal stance. Whether a fiscal tightening will be necessary to disinflate further will depend on its contribution to reducing aggregate demand pressures. In many cases, however, the priority will be structural fiscal reform, including second-generation reforms aimed at fostering economic growth and medium-term fiscal credibility. Key issues will be the structure and level of taxation, social spending, and social transfers. Progress in these areas can benefit disinflation not only by strengthening the fiscal balances, but also by spurring productivity growth.

Policy Response: Credibility-Enhancing Devices

Various monetary frameworks, external agents, and incomes policies were adopted to bolster credibility. This section describes and discusses these devices and assesses their contribution to disinflation.

Monetary Frameworks

A striking feature of the 1993–97 inflation stabilizations is the limited use of formal exchange rate or monetary targets. Though both monetary aggregates and exchange rates did stabilize during and after inflation stabilization (Table 9), the announcement of targets for these variables played a limited

---

[17]Furthermore, receipts from privatization can also ease the solvency condition, especially when privatization greatly increases the productivity of the privatized assets.

Table 9. Broad Money Growth and Depreciation Rates in Transition Economies[1]
(End of period, in percent)

	Broad Money						Depreciation					
	1992	1993	1994	1995	1996	1997	1992	1993	1994	1995	1996	1997
Albania	152.7	75.0	40.6	51.8	43.8	28.4	273.1	5.1	-5.7	-0.9	7.3	47.2
Bulgaria	...	53.5	77.9	39.6	117.9	359.3	14.2	28.9	104.9	7.2	556.4	285.1
Croatia	...	...	72.6	41.3	49.4	37.7	...	839.0	-11.0	-6.7	3.3	13.2
Czech Republic	...	...	19.9	19.8	9.2	10.1	0.0	4.2	-5.1	-5.6	2.5	27.1
Hungary	27.3	16.8	13.0	18.5	20.9	23.2	8.0	20.6	11.6	24.6	17.7	23.0
Macedonia, FYR	...	1,123.0	43.3	10.1	2.3	13.1	5,426.3	277.1	-2.8	-7.3	5.3	36.4
Poland	57.5	36.0	38.4	34.6	29.5	28.9	39.0	37.0	15.3	3.2	13.9	23.4
Romania	75.4	143.3	138.1	71.6	66.0	104.8	132.4	163.6	55.5	44.2	46.0	113.2
Slovak Republic	...	...	18.5	21.2	16.6	8.8	0.1	15.4	-4.7	-5.6	6.3	9.5
Slovenia	121.3	62.4	44.6	29.1	22.2	...	...	34.5	-1.0	-1.9	12.4	18.7
Armenia	41.5	1,444.1	726.9	129.7	34.2	8.6	...	3,523.2	449.3	-2.1	9.9	11.9
Azerbaijan	265.6	685.8	486.1	122.2	25.8	29.8	...	427.4	1,589.4	2.5	-7.7	-5.1
Belarus[2]	482.0	572.6	1,321.5	325.7	66.7	102.8	7,767.9	1,835.3	1,262.8	214.5	15.3	97.1
Estonia	196.3	57.8	29.6	31.3	36.8	40.3	...	7.0	-10.3	-7.4	8.5	15.3
Georgia	416.4	1,225.4	2,055.8	319.4	38.2	35.4	218.8	24,580.3	1,151.2	-3.9	3.6	2.4
Kazakhstan	482.1	581.0	540.2	113.7	20.9	...	...	688.7	759.9	17.9	15.4	2.8
Kyrgyz Republic	...	151.3	139.6	86.9	17.5	20.4	...	...	32.0	5.2	49.8	4.1
Latvia	...	109.3	45.8	-25.7	17.8	...	247.3	2.1	2.6	0.0	0.0	0.0
Lithuania	...	177.0	61.9	31.9	-1.5	...	...	-28.7	-7.9	-2.0	3.5	6.1
Moldova	356.1	256.2	128.3	65.1	15.3	34.0	143.8	778.2	17.3	5.4	3.4	0.2
Russia	505.9	435.9	195.6	129.0	33.1	...	...	200.8	184.7	30.7	19.8	7.2
Tajikistan	513.8	1,587.4	156.3	...	142.8	110.7	...	200.5	184.7	644.1	11.8	127.7
Turkmenistan	960.0	871.7	985.4	448.0	428.8	78.4	...	...	...	166.7	1,935.0	2.3
Ukraine	776.4	1,556.7	467.3	147.1	42.8	42.2	43,446.5	3,237.8	316.8	72.2	5.3	0.5
Uzbekistan	...	987.0	585.6	163.4	113.3	37.0	...	201.2	1,904.8	42.0	54.9	45.7

Source: IMF staff estimates.

[1]The depreciation rates are computed vis-à-vis the U.S. dollar. For the countries that stabilized during 1993–97, shaded areas indicate years in which inflation was below the stabilization threshold (as defined in Table 2).

[2]The depreciation rates refer to the official exchange rate.

role: no country announced monetary targets (although several IMF supported programs included indicative targets on base money) and, perhaps surprisingly, few announced exchange rate targets when initiating disinflation.

The absence of publicly announced monetary targets, other than rules directly implied by the exchange rate regime as in the case of currency boards, reflects structural change and uncertainty. Reform in the financial sector—particularly the advent of substitutes for bank deposits for household savings and innovations in payment systems—was substantial. This compounded the lack of knowledge of money demand and the prospect that disinflation itself would induce a strong, though unpredictable, recovery in real money demand. In this context, money targets appeared to be unworkable as signals for inflation expectation formation.[18]

Exchange rate targets—the most obvious substitute for monetary targets—were initially adopted only by a handful of countries (Tables 10 and 11). They subsequently became more common: by 1997, the share of floaters had dropped to little more than one-half, and was thus close to the share of floaters in nontransition developing countries in the mid-1990s (Cottarelli and Giannini, 1997). Note that, in the most recent period (1995–97), the increase in the number of pegs reflects the increased popularity of broad band pegs. Former floaters, such as Russia and the Ukraine, as well as former narrow band pegs, such as Poland and the Slovak Republic, have shifted to this intermediate regime.[19] In contrast, only the Czech Republic has crossed the whole spectrum from a peg to a managed float.

[18]See Begg, Hesselman, and Smith (1996), and Begg (1998) for Central and Eastern European countries, and De Broeck, Krajnyák,

and Lorie (1997) for the Baltics, Russia, and other countries of the former Soviet Union. Van Elkan (1998) discusses the case of Hungary. Anderson and Citrin (1995) discuss the response of money demand to inflation.

[19]Russia floated in August 1998.

Table 10. Number of Peggers and Floaters[1]

	1992	1993	1994	1995	1996	1997
Peggers						
Central and Eastern European countries	3	3	5	5	3	4
Baltics, Russia, and other countries of the former Soviet Union	1	1	3	3	3	3
Total	4	4	8	8	6	7
Broad band peggers						
Central and Eastern European countries	—	—	—	1	3	2
Baltics, Russia, and other countries of the former Soviet Union	—	—	—	1	1	2
Total	—	—	—	2	4	4
Floaters						
Central and Eastern European countries	7	7	5	4	4	4
Baltics, Russia, and other countries of the former Soviet Union	14	14	12	11	11	10
Total	21	21	17	15	15	14

Source: IMF staff reports.

[1]In this table, the exchange regime of the countries that had not yet introduced their own currency is the exchange regime of the preexisting currency.

Among the successful inflation stabilizations between 1993–97, only Bulgaria (in 1997), Lithuania, Estonia, and the former Yugoslav Republic of Macedonia formally pegged throughout, though Russia adopted a broad band a few months after the beginning of its disinflation program.[20] Croatia announced an exchange rate floor against the deutsche mark and allowed the nominal exchange rate to appreciate initially, although most now consider that it is operating a de facto peg. Even in the four disinflations that occurred without a fiscal tightening, where weaknesses in the nominal anchor framework might have been thought to have been sustaining inflation, only Estonia used a formal exchange rate anchor to stabilize expectations. Latvia, Turkmenistan, and Ukraine formally floated (in the latter two cases, throughout).

The role of different exchange regimes in disinflation remains under dispute. Bruno (1992) concluded that exchange rate anchors had played a key role in the early disinflation cases, and is supported by econometric evidence for that period (Fischer,

Sahay, and Végh, 1996; and Cottarelli, Griffiths, and Moghadam, 1998). However, others, focusing on more recent disinflations, have argued that formal exchange rate anchors were not critical for disinflation (Zettermeyer and Citrin, 1995; Budina and van Wijnbergen, 1997; Begg, 1998; and Gomulka, 1998). Indeed, in two-thirds of the inflation stabilization cases observed during 1993–97, the exchange rate was formally floating (Table 11).[21]

The popularity of exchange rate floats during the later inflation stabilization episodes is striking, particularly in light of the role pegs were thought capable of playing as "launching vehicles" for new fiat monies lacking an initial credibility endowment (Selgin, 1994), their high visibility and direct effect on prices through imported inflation, despite the absence of sensible monetary anchors as alternatives. Most of these countries followed what in essence were discretionary monetary frameworks, or informal inflation targeting regimes.[22]

Not only has evidence of successful inflation stabilization with formally floating exchange rates mounted, but there is no clear evidence that these episodes have involved a higher sacrifice ratio. Indeed, if anything, the converse appears to be the case. The ratio between percentage change in output and percentage change in inflation during the disinflation year and in the following year is larger for countries with a pegged exchange rate than in the group of floaters, and this pattern is apparent even allowing for other determinants of growth (Christoffersen and Doyle, 1998).

There are various possible accounts of the declining frequency of formal pegs during disinflation in transition: that the disinflations after 1993 tended to confront more extreme inflations with less inflation inertia and so the credibility-enhancing role of formal pegs was less important; that informal pegging was both relatively frequent and proved to be a close substitute for formal pegs even in these higher disinflation cases; and that there were a number of practical "entry and exit" issues that qualified the general case for formal exchange rate pegs during disinflation.

Clearly, the inflation stabilizations after 1993 included a greater number of cases of extreme inflation than earlier (Table 1). Accordingly, the credibility-enhancing role of formal pegs may have been less important to effective disinflation than in earlier

---

[20]In Table 11, the former Yugoslav Republic of Macedonia is classified as having a pegged exchange rate because the authorities announced their commitment to a certain exchange rate level. Croatia is similarly classified because it announced an exchange rate floor at the beginning of the disinflation.

[21]Latvia introduced a fixed exchange rate some 18 months after initiating stabilization.

[22]Transition economies have only recently begun to consider and to adopt formal inflation targeting frameworks. The Czech Republic adopted this framework informally in late 1997, and formalized it in early 1998. Poland introduced inflation targeting in late 1998.

Table 11. Exchange Rate Regime in Transition Countries

	1992	1993	1994	1995	1996	1997
Albania	Floating	Floating	Floating	Floating	Floating	Floating
Bulgaria	Floating	Floating	Floating	Floating	Floating	Currency board[1]
Croatia[2]	Floating	Floating	Peg	Peg	Peg	Peg
Czech Republic	Peg	Peg	Peg	Peg	Broad band peg[3]	Managed float[4]
Hungary	Managed float	Managed float	Managed float	Crawling peg[5]	Crawling peg	Crawling peg
Macedonia, FYR	Managed float	Managed float	Peg	Peg	Peg	Peg
Poland	Crawling peg	Crawling peg	Crawling peg	Broad band crawling peg[6]	Broad band crawling peg	Broad band crawling peg
Romania	Managed float	Managed float	Managed float	Managed float	Managed float	Managed float
Slovak Republic	Peg	Peg	Peg	Peg	Broad band peg	Broad band peg
Slovenia	Managed float	Managed float	Managed float	Managed float	Managed float	Managed float
Armenia	No national currency	No national currency	Managed float[7]	Managed float	Managed float	Managed float
Azerbaijan	No national currency	No national currency	Floating[8]	Floating	Floating	Floating
Belarus	No national currency	No national currency	Managed float	Peg	Managed float	Managed float
Estonia	Currency board	Currency board	Currency board	Currency board	Currency board	Currency board
Georgia	No national currency	Managed float[9]	Managed float	Managed float	Managed float	Managed float
Kazakhstan	No national currency	No national currency	Managed float	Managed float	Managed float	Managed float
Kyrgyz Republic	No national currency	Managed float	Managed float	Managed float	Managed float	Managed float
Latvia	Floating	Floating	Peg[10]	Peg	Peg	Peg
Lithuania	Floating	Floating	Currency board[11]	Currency board	Currency board	Currency board
Moldova	No national currency	No national currency	Floating[12]	Managed float	Managed float	Managed float
Russia	Floating	Floating	Floating	Broad band peg[13]	Broad band crawling peg	Broad band crawling peg

(continued on next page)

cases because inflation inertia was more limited. Thus, to the extent that sustained exchange rate stability signified the elimination of the excess monetary growth at the root of these later inflations, it may have been more important that the exchange rate was stabilized than that this was achieved by means of a credibility-enhancing formal exchange rate commitment.

It is more difficult to assess the role of informal pegging—that is, exchange rate stabilization through intervention or adjustment in monetary instruments in the context of a formally floating regime. The stability of the nominal exchange rate in several transition economies with formally floating exchange rates after the inflation stabilization was notable, including for example, in Armenia and the Kyrgyz Republic in 1995 during their disinflations, and in Georgia from 1995 through 1997. However, while the exchange rate was closely monitored in all countries, it appears that only in relatively few cases, such as Moldova, Slovenia, and occasionally Kazakhstan, were intervention and monetary instruments focused on informal exchange rate targets as part of the policy framework underlying disinflation. And even acknowledging such cases, it remains remarkable that so few countries adopted formal exchange rate targets.

The declining incidence of formal pegs also reflects concerns about entry and exit issues (Gomulka, 1998; Begg, 1998; and IMF, 1997, pp. 114–15). On the entry side, many countries in the post-1993 period began their disinflations with low international reserves, and so may not have been able to operate pegs credibly at sensible exchange rates. The mirror image of this problem, on the exit side, was the risk for a country of entering the ex-

Table 11 *(concluded)*

	1992	1993	1994	1995	1996	1997
Tajikistan	No national currency	No national currency	No national currency	Floating[14]	Floating	Floating
Turkmenistan	No national currency	No national currency	Managed float[15]	Managed float	Managed float	Peg
Ukraine	No national currency	Managed float[16]	Managed float	Floating[17]	Floating	Broad band peg
Uzbekistan	No national currency	No national currency	Managed float	Managed float	Managed float	Managed float

Source: IMF staff reports.

Notes: The exchange rate is regarded as floating in the absence of major exchange rate intervention; managed float means that some intervention takes place but the exchange rate is not regarded as the main monetary anchor; exchange regimes in which the exchange rate peg is frequently revised (as in Hungary before March 1995) are also classified as managed float; pegged exchange rates are formal pegs or regimes in which the authorities have, at least in some periods, announced their commitment to a certain exchange rate target and the exchange rate is regarded as pegged by most market participants. The term "crawling peg" refers to regimes in which the rate of exchange rate depreciation is preannounced. For the countries that stabilized during 1993–97, shaded areas indicate the years in which inflation was below the stabilization threshold (as defined in Table 2).

[1] As of July 1, 1997.

[2] In 1992–93, the exchange rate was repeatedly devalued (being formally floated between May and October 1993). In October 1993, an exchange rate floor (maximum depreciation) was announced; after a brief period of appreciation, the exchange rate stabilized.

[3] As of February 28, 1996.

[4] As of May 27, 1997.

[5] As of March 15, 1995.

[6] As of May 1995.

[7] As of November 22, 1993.

[8] During the first quarter of 1994, the exchange rate was pegged to the U.S. dollar; in April and May 1994, it was pegged to the ruble.

[9] The Georgian coupon was introduced in April 1993, and the lari was introduced in September 1995.

[10] As of February 1994.

[11] As of April 1994.

[12] As of November 1993.

[13] As of July 1995.

[14] National currency introduced in May 1995.

[15] National currency introduced on November 1, 1993.

[16] National currency introduced in March 1993.

[17] As of October 1994.

change rate peg at a substantially undervalued exchange rate. Pegging at such rates might have slowed inflation from its extremely high levels initially. But thereafter, it could have implied ongoing inflation above partner country levels to correct the real exchange rate, compounding similar pressures for this arising from relatively rapid productivity growth in the tradable sector (the Balassa-Samuelson effect).[23] And pegs, in the context of moderate inflation, might also induce large short-term capital inflows.

These difficulties with pegs as nominal anchors for disinflation took a particular form in a number of the BRO countries in the mid-1990s. Disinflation using pegs normally requires that the peg is set against a low inflation hard currency, such as the deutsche mark or the dollar, or a hard currency basket. However, the fact that Russia was a major trading partner for the Baltics and for the countries of the former Soviet Union created a dilemma for this approach to setting a peg in those countries. To eliminate shocks to competitiveness and inflation arising from changes in the real exchange rate of the ruble, the latter would need to be included among the currencies defining the peg. But this would have weakened the ex ante credibility of the peg as a nominal anchor because the ruble was so vulnerable. Hence, the uncertain prospects for the ruble in the mid-1990s qualified the merits of hard currency pegs as nominal anchors for the disinflation efforts elsewhere in the BRO countries.

The various difficulties with pegs are illustrated in the experience of transition countries that stabilized inflation both before and after 1993. After initial successes, advanced pegging reformers, notably the

---

[23] Transition factors have been found to add to the speed of real appreciation in oil-rich countries of the Baltics, Russia, and other countries of the former Soviet Union, such as Azerbaijan (Rosenberg and Saavalainen, 1998).

Czech Republic, Estonia, Hungary, Latvia, Lithuania, and Poland have made slow progress toward low inflation while they have retained their pegs. The inflationary pressures arising from an undervalued peg are illustrated by the kroon, the level of which at the outset of disinflation implied wages in Estonia of about one-seventh of those in Poland. Latvia is also thought to have pegged too low, despite its initial float (Hansson, 1997), and inflation above industrial country levels was slow to correct this undervaluation (Richards and Tersman, 1995). The recovery of the ruble between 1994–96 in real terms may have delayed the correction of the Latvian undervaluation further. In other cases (notably Hungary and Poland), rates of crawl in 1996–97 may have come to imply floors rather than ceilings on inflation because the authorities were unwilling to use the rate of crawl as an active disinflation tool, given the *uncertainty* about the real equilibrium exchange rate and their past exposure to external shocks. Difficulties in managing capital flows—most clear in the case of the Czech Republic up to 1997—may partly account for the recent trend toward broad band pegs.

The advantages of discretionary monetary frameworks are illustrated by Albania, Azerbaijan, and Georgia, and for some months after the start of their disinflations, Croatia and Russia. In these cases, rapid disinflation was accompanied by nominal appreciation of the exchange rate, correcting an initial undervaluation. In all these cases, appreciation boosted the disinflating effects of lower import prices compared to a peg, facilitating an even faster disinflation.[24] Moreover, in some countries, the nominal exchange rate appreciation, after years of continuous depreciation, signaled a clear break with the past, with a dramatic impact in inflation expectations (Škreb, 1998).

It should be recognized that a nominal appreciation of the exchange rate involves some risks. Unless prices and wages adjust rapidly to changes in the nominal exchange rate, a nominal appreciation will lead to a real appreciation. As noted, a real appreciation may be consistent with fundamentals in transition economies characterized by high productivity growth, or in case of an initial undervaluation. But whether this is the case or not in practice is a judgment call, involving a wide margin of uncertainty, particularly taking into account dynamic factors. In practice, it may be difficult for the authorities to assess whether a real appreciation following a nominal appreciation reflects sluggishness in wage and price adjustment, with a negative impact at least in the short run on the external accounts, rather than an equilibrium appreciation. These considerations may be more important at moderate inflation levels, at which wage and price stickiness may be stronger. Indeed, the authorities of some moderate inflation countries have justified their reluctance to abandon exchange rate crawling pegs with the risks arising from such a move for external equilibrium (Section III).

The disinflations achieved under discretionary monetary regimes—similar to informal inflation targeting—are notable given the cautious assessment given to more fully fledged inflation targeting regimes in developing countries (Masson, Savastano, and Sharma, 1997). The low inertia in the initial inflation being stabilized—a key difference with respect to Latin American disinflation episodes—the drawbacks of monetary and exchange rate targets in the transition context, the focus on fiscal consolidation, and the credibility gained from increased central bank independence and the adoption of IMF-supported programs may account for these successes. In most cases, however, the performance of discretionary monetary frameworks has yet to stand the test of time.

Credibility Through Delegation

Central bank independence and IMF-supported programs featured in many of the inflation stabilizations, and may have buttressed financial discipline and the credibility of the disinflation programs. During 1993–97, most transition economies enhanced the legal independence of their central banks (Knight, 1997; and Radzyner and Riesinger, 1997)—price stability is now the main mandated objective of central banks in most transition economies; and ceilings on central bank credit to the government have been tightened, with many countries having prohibited any credit to the government (Table 12). There has also been significant progress in extending the terms of central bank governors, the rules for their appointment and revocation, as well as in strengthening the financial independence of the central bank.

A survey of IMF desk economists used in Cottarelli, Griffiths, and Moghadam (1998) provides a summary indicator of this trend. Desk economists were asked to rate central bank independence in terms of control on monetary policy instruments, constraints on credit to the government, statutory mandate, and ability of the government to dismiss the central bank governor. On a 1–10 scale (10 being the maximum degree of cen-

---

[24]This factor played a role in the Baltics and in the countries of the former Soviet Union closely integrated with Russia as its real exchange rate rebounded during 1994–96. In this context, such countries that did not respond to the ruble appreciation with offsetting appreciations against "hard" currencies experienced substantial overall real effective depreciations, and consequently high import price inflation. This delayed disinflation.

Table 12. Developments in Central Bank Legislation

	Major Revision of Central Bank Legislation	Main Objective of the Central Bank	Credit to the Government Constraints on Central Bank
Albania	1998	Price stability	Percentage of revenues in the previous year[1]
Bulgaria	1997	Currency board	No credit
Croatia	1992[2]	Stability of national currency and payment liquidity	5 percent of budget revenue, repayable within the year
Czech Republic	1992	Stability of the national currency	5 percent of previous year's state budget revenue
Hungary	1996	Internal and external value of the currency	Small liquidity facility
Macedonia, FYR	1992	Safeguard the value of the currency	5 percent of budgeted revenues
Poland	1997	Price stability	No credit (constitutional law)
Romania	1998	Currency and price stability	7 percent of revenues in the previous year
Slovak Republic	1992[3]	Stability of the currency	5 percent of revenues in the previous year
Slovenia	...	Currency stability and general liquidity of payments	One-fifth of budgeted deficit
Armenia	1996	Price stability	
Azerbaijan	1996	Price stability (as one objective)	No constraint
Belarus	1995	...	...
Estonia	1992	Currency board	No credit
Georgia	1995	Price stability	...
Kazakhstan	1997	Internal and external stability of the currency	No credit
Kyrgyz Republic	1997	Price stability	No credit
Latvia	1992	Exchange rate peg	...
Lithuania	1994	Currency board	No credit
Moldova	1995	Stability of the national currency	Amount agreed in annual state budget
Russia	1995	Price stability (as one objective)	...
Tajikistan	1996	...	...
Turkmenistan	1993	Price stability (as one objective)	8 percent of normal budget revenue over past three years
Ukraine	1997	Monetary stability	...
Uzbekistan	1995	Stability of the national currency	No constraint

Source: IMF staff estimates.

[1]The percentage declined sharply starting in 1998.

[2]A new draft is in preparation.

[3]A new central bank law was submitted to Parliament in 1997, but was later withdrawn. The draft was regarded to weaken the independence of the central bank.

tral bank independence), the average rating of CEE transition economies moved from 4.7 in 1993 to 5.3 in 1996. The average in the Baltics, Russia, and other countries of the former Soviet Union (excluding those with currency boards) also improved from 4.7 to 8.4 in the same period.[25] Further progress was made in 1997 and in 1998 in several countries, including Albania, Hungary, Kazakhstan, the Kyrgyz Republic, and Poland. However, attempts—unsuccessful so far—have been made to weaken the central bank law in the Slovak Republic. Moreover, central bank credit to the government—possibly the most important indicator of central bank independence—remains unrestricted in a number of the Baltics, Russia, and other countries of the former Soviet Union (Table 12).

---

[25]As indices reflect subjective views, they should be taken as indicative of direction of change, rather than of relative positions across countries. Following more rigorous methodology—which focuses only on legal independence—Cukierman, Miller, and Neyapti (1998) conclude that the level of legal independence of transition economies is even higher than in developed economies and is broadly the same on average for the Baltics, Russia, and other countries of the former Soviet Union and Central and Eastern European countries.

Some econometric studies shed some light on the importance of central bank independence in transition (Cottarelli, Griffiths, and Moghadam, 1998; and Lougani and Sheets, 1997). Controlling for other factors, inflation is lower in countries with more independent central banks. Cukierman, Miller, and Neyapti (1998) find that central bank independence is unrelated to inflation during the early stages of liberalization, but it reduces inflation for sufficiently high levels of liberalization.

With only three exceptions—Croatia, Slovenia, and Turkmenistan—the inflation stabilizations of 1993–97 took place in the presence of IMF-supported programs; in seven cases, under the Systemic Transformation Facility, but more frequently under other IMF arrangements. And even in these three cases, the authorities maintained a dialogue with the IMF. The incidence of IMF-supported programs suggests that they were regarded as an important component of the disinflation effort throughout the transition area. However, with almost all countries following IMF-supported programs, it is virtually impossible to conduct statistical tests of the marginal impact of IMF-assistance on shaping appropriate policies or strengthening the credibility of those policies.

Incomes Policies

Some countries also employed incomes policies, though their contribution to disinflation is disputed. Though they featured in various forms in many initial disinflations, it is difficult to identify their contribution to real or nominal wage adjustments or inflation, after controlling for other influences on these variables (Morsink, 1995).

The approaches ranged from excess wage taxes (Belarus, Estonia, Latvia, Poland, Romania, and Slovakia) through formal wage guidelines or controls for the public and private sectors (as in Croatia, Hungary, Lithuania, and the former Yugoslav Republic of Macedonia) to wage limits applied only in the public sector with the aim of influencing private wage setting by example (Albania and Moldova). Several countries, however, did not use any form of incomes policy, including many of the disinflations of 1994–95 in the Baltics, Russia, and other countries of the former Soviet Union (Azerbaijan, Georgia, Kazakhstan, the Kyrgyz Republic, and Russia). Even in countries where incomes policy was present, it is not regarded as one of the main factors behind disinflation, in some cases because of substantial noncompliance. Incomes policy is regarded to have played an important role only in a handful of Central and Eastern European countries (Albania, Bulgaria, Croatia, and the former Yugoslav Republic of Macedonia).

Blanchard (1998) suggests that incomes policies may not have affected inflation expectations in the transition context because they were often used to secure sizable shifts in income distribution that transition required. Wage growth was set at a level significantly below what inflation turned out to be, in this way leading to a sharp drop in real wages. While this adjustment was inevitable, it undermined the subsequent use of incomes policy as a tool of fast disinflation. A case in point is Hungary, in which a tight wage policy in 1995–96 resulted in a sharp contraction of real wages (inflation being sustained by the exchange rate depreciation in early 1995 and needed increases in administered prices). This undermined the credibility of incomes policy in 1997, and partly explains the lack of progress in inflation during that year. Finally, the resulting shifts in the distribution of income secured by the incomes policies weakened tax revenues in cases where the taxation of labor was more onerous or effective than the taxation of nonlabor income. Concern with the consequent loss of revenue may at times have qualified the authorities' commitment to incomes policies. This was particularly apparent in Poland in 1990–91, where this incentive was compounded by tax receipts derived from the excess wage tax.

Policy Response: Sequencing and Speed

The final characteristic of the policies that appears to have contributed to the absence of evidence of output costs arising from disinflation concerns the sequencing of disinflation relative to structural reform and its intended speed.

Much theoretical reasoning about the relative sequencing of disinflation and structural reform was predicated on moderate inflation, and much of it advocated structural reform first, as a condition to enhance the credibility of disinflation. Blanchard (1998) suggests that disinflation is easier when it is purely a matter of inflation coordination, and is not accompanied by structural changes in relative prices and wages. Szapáry (1998) notes that inflation, in the presence of money illusion, may be needed to implement structural relative price changes, such as a redistribution from wages to profits. The findings of Berg and others (1998) on the differential impact of inflation on the public and private sector suggests that inflation should fall as the private sector expands. Kornai (1998) emphasizes that the behavior of unreformed economies is highly uncertain. So structural reform should precede disinflation, both to render macroeconomic developments during disinflation more predictable and to provide an offsetting underlying growth stimulus to any recessionary trend during disinflation.

Theoretical arguments favoring the reverse sequencing in a moderate inflation context are relatively few. They include that structural measures take so long that postponed disinflation risks entrenching inflation expectations (Cottarelli and Szapáry, 1998). Burton and Fischer (1998) add that the timing of disinflation should, in part, be opportunistic. It should exploit favorable supply shocks and political openings when they occur, rather than necessarily waiting for structural reforms or other desirable preconditions to be in place.

In practice, inflation stabilization in the Central and Eastern European countries was accompanied by a burst of structural reform, a pattern not evident in the Baltics, Russia, and other countries of the former Soviet Union (Figure 1). Nevertheless, by the third year of stabilization, both country groups had made similar structural progress. These patterns rarely reflected a sophisticated choice. Structural reforms inevitably take time, and particularly in the Baltics, Russia, and other countries of the former Soviet Union, inflation was so extreme that it clearly had to be addressed first. This may partly explain why political or technical trade-offs between disinflation and structural reform were apparent in only a few countries. For successful stabilizers such as Armenia, Croatia, and Ukraine, the precedence given to disinflation reflected its urgency, not that structural reform was sacrificed to disinflation or that disinflation was substituted for structural reform. In Hungary, however, the authorities argued that simultaneous disinflation and structural reform would have been politically impossible (Surányi and Vincze, 1998): as inflation was moderate, precedence was given to structural reform. The political difficulty of implementing structural reform and aggressive disinflation at the same time has also been stressed in the case of Romania.

While comprehensive structural reform was not a precondition for inflation stabilization in most cases, minimal progress may have been necessary, notably the establishment of a "hard-budget constraint" environment and the associated termination of inter-enterprise and tax arrears. The failure of some disin-

---

Box 3. Disinflation Reversals in 1993–97: Albania, Bulgaria, and Romania

Albania, Bulgaria, and Romania stand out as cases where substantial disinflation was reversed.[1] In 1995, Albania had reduced 12-month inflation to 6 percent, and Bulgaria and Romania had reduced inflation to below 35 percent. But by the end of 1997, inflation had increased to 40 percent, 580 percent, and 150 percent, respectively.

Albania made substantial progress between 1993–95, with forceful privatization, large cuts in public employment, rapid disinflation, and strong output growth. Though electoral pressures were reflected in a deteriorating fiscal position in 1996, and some increase in inflation, the emergence and rapid growth of pyramid schemes operating on an unprecedented scale ultimately led to the financial crisis and public disorder of early 1997, and to the resurgence of inflation. Problems in Bulgaria were more long-standing. Structural reform was intermittent and uneven since 1990. Combined with political instability, this bolstered the rent-seeking culture, undermined fiscal policy, and culminated in economic crises in 1994, 1996, and in hyperinflation in early 1997. Stop-go policy has been only slightly less marked in Romania. The political commitment to the agricultural and energy sectors has pervaded all aspects of policy, from privatization and price liberalization to the exchange rate, undermining all initiatives to implement sustained structural and fiscal reform.

Chronic financial fragility, revealed in the collapses of banks and pyramid schemes, is a common feature of all three cases. And, while all three cases illustrate how long even much abused financial sectors can survive, they also demonstrate how costly delayed financial sector reform can ultimately turn out to be. Financial fragility also reflected other underlying structural weaknesses. In Bulgaria, widespread soft-budget constraints in industry undermined disinflation. In Romania, inflation largely reflected support of energy and farming, with weaknesses in the banking sector being less directly important. However, central bank support to two banks at the end of 1997 led to a significant monetary relaxation. The immediate cause of the surge of inflation in Albania was civil disorder, but the root cause of this was inadequate control of unlicensed deposit takers.

Fiscal indiscipline also undermined disinflation. In 1997, large quasi-fiscal deficits persisted after the disinflation. The ratio of the overall fiscal deficit to GDP in Albania has remained in double digits since 1992. And while Bulgaria's primary fiscal balance recorded strong surpluses prior to the reemergence of inflation, heavy quasi-fiscal losses accruing in the financial sector persisted.

---

[1]Uzbekistan also experienced a resurgence of inflation in 1997, from a low point for 12-month inflation of 42 percent in October 1996, to a subsequent high of 82 percent in August 1997, as policies were relaxed following a poor agricultural harvest. However, thus far, this resurgence is not on the same scale as that of the Central and Eastern European countries discussed here.

flation attempts, such as the first two attempts in Russia as well as other BRO countries was in part due to the absence of such an environment.

Structural reform that is insufficiently comprehensive, for example, one that fails to develop effective corporate governance structures, is likely, however, to weaken the chances of maintaining price stability in the long run. As noted in Section III, strong reformers have a lower incentive to inflate and have enjoyed lower inflation. Moreover, it is significant that structural weaknesses—in public enterprises, in the financial system, and in governance structures—were behind the major episodes of inflation reversal during 1993–97 (Albania and Bulgaria after the first disinflation, and Romania; see Box 3). This suggests that those countries of the Baltics, Russia, and other countries of the former Soviet Union that stabilized inflation recently but that have not made more progress on structural reform than those countries that have experienced reversals may have difficulties in sustaining disinflation over time, unless wide-ranging reform is accelerated.

Having decided to stabilize first, most countries attempted to stabilize quickly. This likely helped cred-

ibility, given the high inflation context. As discussed above, when inflation has little inertia, as it generally has at high rates, the short-run output costs of rapid disinflation are usually lower. So a gradual approach risks signaling some lack of intent about disinflation, which undermines credibility. Bulgaria and Romania illustrate this difficulty, while the experience in Azerbaijan, Croatia, and the former Yugoslav Republic of Macedonia is suggestive of how successful such rapid disinflations could have been in these cases. But when inflation has some inertia, as more commonly occurs at less extreme rates, rapid disinflation may be more likely to incur short-run output losses. For this reason, a gradual approach is less likely to suggest a lack of commitment to disinflation because it may reflect appropriate concerns about output. This pattern does not mean that all rapid disinflations of high inflation and gradual disinflations of moderate inflation are credible, nor that the reverse pairings are always noncredible: the Czechoslovak experience in 1991 shows that rapid stabilization of moderately high inflation is possible. But the pattern suggests that gradual stabilization of high inflation and rapid stabilization of moderate inflation may have inherent credibility problems.

V   Persistent Moderate Inflation

Having stabilized inflation rapidly and credibly, a number of advanced transition countries appear to have got stuck with moderate inflation in the 10–30 percent range (see Table 1, Section II, and Figure 4). The Czech Republic and Slovenia have spent 3–4 years in the high single-digit range. The Baltic States have only recently come down to those levels from the 20–40 percent range in 1993–95. Hungary has hovered in the 20–30 percent range throughout transition, until 1998, when it began disinflating into the lower teens from there. And Poland, after its rapid disinflation in 1990–91, has taken six years to get to the low teens. This section considers the factors underlying the slow progress after the initial dramatic successes.

The characteristics of the transition countries that have sustained five or more years of disinflation are highlighted in Figure 4. The key features are as follows: growth resumed in the second year after disinflation was initiated; these are generally "big bang" structural reformers; after five years, the group has institutional characteristics closely resembling those of mature market economies; the group has achieved increasingly strong fiscal positions; and although large current account deficits have appeared, the debt financed component of the external current account deficit has generally been relatively contained, though latterly, with increased variance. Finally, a glance at Table 11 confirms that the group has overwhelmingly pegged their exchange rates or has applied crawling pegs, though the Czech Republic switched to a managed float in 1997, joining Slovenia.

This summary indicates that progress toward price stability halted despite a propitious environment for disinflation: output, the debt-financed external balance, and fiscal policies have been strong, and structural reforms are far advanced. Furthermore, the experience of two countries outside this group—Croatia and the former Yugoslav Republic of Macedonia—confirms that sustained low inflation is clearly possible in the transition context, although further policy adjustments, on both the structural and macroeconomic sides, may be necessary to sustain this performance.

Rather than reflecting a difficult environment for disinflation or an "inflation floor" in transition, the persistent inflation of advanced reformers appears to reflect their choices of exchange rate regime and their policy preferences about inflation. Some advanced moderate inflaters, including the Czech Republic and the Baltic States, were reluctant to abandon successful nominal exchange rate anchors. This commitment persisted even if initial undervaluation, reductions in underlying country risk premiums, and large relative price and relative productivity changes required real appreciations of their currencies. Clearly, in these circumstances, nominal appreciations would have been necessary to effect real exchange rate corrections with lower inflation. Persistent moderate inflation in the Baltic States appears to derive most clearly from this source (Richards and Tersman, 1995), compounded by the real effective appreciation of the ruble between 1994 and 1997. Paradoxically, after the initial stabilizations of inflation, further reductions toward industrial country rates may have been delayed by the commitment of these countries to nominal anchors that were intended to signal adherence to prudent policies. Mutatis mutandis, the same argument applies to countries with a crawling peg where the rate of crawl may have been lowered too gradually to avoid the risk of a real appreciation.

But the persistence of moderate inflation also reflected perceived trade-offs. Having reduced inflation to well below its recent peaks and to levels that international investors and the authorities perceived as "low by transition standards," some moderate inflaters saw no urgency to progress further. And some also feared that further progress would require output losses on top of those that had accompanied the initial stages of transition (Medgyessy, 1998). Thus, for example, Hungary prioritized structural reforms and reduced the external current account deficit and external debt after 1995 over further disinflation.

Finally, administered price adjustments often bulk large in relative price changes: typically, rents and utility prices have been held artificially low, and these sectors generally have limited scope for productivity gains to ease supply constraints. The con-

Figure 4. Advanced Transition Reformers, 1990–97

(In disinflation time)[1,2]

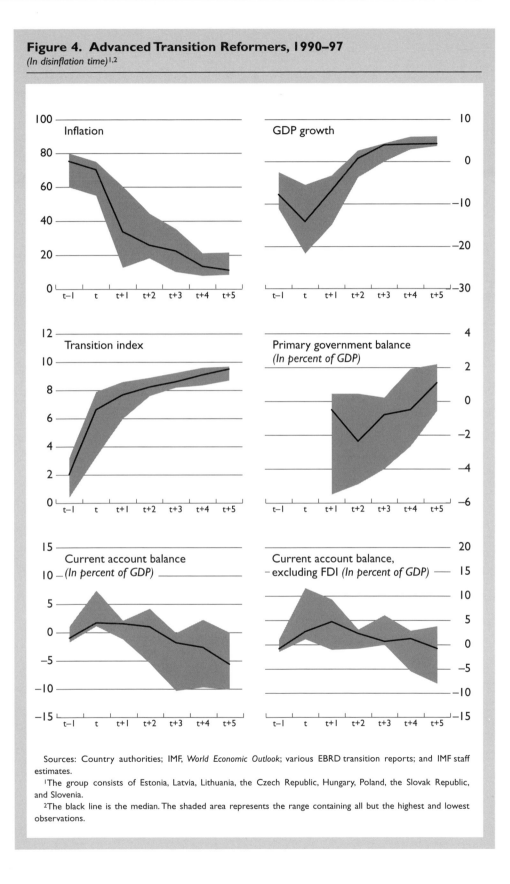

Sources: Country authorities; IMF, *World Economic Outlook*; various EBRD transition reports; and IMF staff estimates.

[1]The group consists of Estonia, Latvia, Lithuania, the Czech Republic, Hungary, Poland, the Slovak Republic, and Slovenia.

[2]The black line is the median. The shaded area represents the range containing all but the highest and lowest observations.

sequent relative price adjustments have boosted headline CPI rates, with an impact that is particularly evident in moderate inflation contexts where relative price adjustments automatically loom larger. Accordingly, moderate inflaters that "backloaded" administrative price adjustments in their reform programs, including the Czech Republic, report higher headline CPI rates. Nevertheless, even underlying inflation rates have remained persistently above industrial country levels in these cases.

Persistent moderate inflation among advanced transition countries thus appears to reflect policy choices rather than structural features of transition.

Those choices had various elements, including concerns about abandoning hitherto successful nominal anchors, the risks further disinflation might imply for output, and a perception that sufficient progress on inflation had already been made. These choices are changing, however. Many of the authorities in the group believe now that reducing inflation to industrial country levels is both feasible and desirable. These views are reflected in their accession programs to the European Union, and in recent reforms of exchange rate regimes, including the shift to formal inflation targeting in the Czech Republic and in Poland.

VI Conclusions

The reduction in inflation since the early 1990s right across the transition area is remarkable, particularly given the chaotic conditions at the outset. Inflationary pressures that had long been suppressed by price controls turned out to be one of the lesser challenges, as nascent policymaking institutions wrestled with collapsing output, employment, and fiscal revenues, as well as military conflicts and redrawn national boundaries. In such conditions, most currencies, new and old, collapsed, and inflation surged. But these difficulties notwithstanding, disinflation has been achieved throughout the region. Once undertaken, it was swift and there is no systematic evidence that it compounded output losses. Furthermore, major resurgences of inflation have been the exception. And in this lower inflation environment, growth has resumed, with formal evidence suggesting a direct link between reduced inflation and the resumption of growth.

The robustness of output during disinflation reflects three factors.

- The context for disinflation was better than it appeared: in the highest inflation cases, there was little inertia in prices and political support for disinflation was often strong; financial fragility rarely deepened during disinflation; and after the hurdle of initial relative price adjustment, price liberalization helped.
- Inflation stabilization was implemented first, without waiting for the completion of all-encompassing structural reforms, and it was intended to be rapid.
- Comprehensive fiscal consolidation underwrote disinflation, and funding sources were diversified through the development of financial markets.

Just as collapsing tax revenues, rigid expenditures, and limited financing options had forced heavy reliance on seigniorage—notably in the Baltics, Russia, and other countries of the former Soviet Union in the early 1990s—so fundamental fiscal adjustments, usually focused on expenditure cuts, underlay disinflation. However, inflation stabilization did not require "fiscal solvency," as defined by a primary surplus sufficiently high as to stabilize the public debt-to-GDP ratio. This is probably because dynamic solvency (the prospective evolution of the primary balance), rather than a snapshot of the primary balance, matters more in an environment characterized by deep structural changes. In addition, the relationship between fiscal adjustment and disinflation becomes more blurred at moderate inflation levels, when inflation is likely to be driven more by expectations than by fundamentals.

The role of monetary frameworks in strengthening disinflations is more controversial. Some, perhaps surprisingly few, countries adopted formal exchange rate pegs as their principal nominal anchors, especially in the disinflations after 1993. Most formally floated, though some of these pegged informally at times. Those that pegged throughout generally stabilized relatively rapidly but also experienced persistent moderate inflation, despite firm fiscal adjustment. The latter reflected Belassa-Samuelson effects and the correction of undervalued pegs through inflation above international levels, and was accommodated by capital inflows whenever domestic sources of monetary growth were restrictive. In some cases where fiscal adjustment accompanied an initial appreciation of the nominal exchange rate, such as Croatia and the former Yugoslav Republic of Macedonia, disinflation was more rapid and low inflation was sustained. Both formal floaters and countries that pegged their exchange rates attempted to boost the credibility of their chosen monetary frameworks by deepening the independence of their central banks and by disinflating in the context of IMF-supported programs.

The progress made in reducing inflation should not obscure the fact that the achievements are—with few notable exceptions—not long-standing. Even aside from the major inflation reversals (including Russia during the summer of 1998), a number of countries have experienced some resurgence of inflation (Armenia, Belarus, and Uzbekistan), and in some cases (Belarus and Uzbekistan), price controls on basic consumer goods have recently been intensified. It would be premature to presume that labor markets and financial markets in transition economies now generally discount a low inflation environment. For this reason alone, policymakers that are perceived to believe that inflation has fallen far enough are at risk of losing control of inflation once again. This risk is even evident in countries that experienced persistent moderate inflation, where inflation has repeatedly exceeded official targets, albeit within manageable margins thus far.

But even where a moderate inflation environment is reasonably assured, there is much to commend more ambitious goals—to lower inflation to industrial country levels soon. The estimated threshold above which inflation involves significant output costs appears to be close to industrial country inflation rates for fully fledged market economies, and this provides the relevant benchmark for the most advanced transition economies, including the Czech Republic, Estonia, Hungary, and Poland. With sizable relative price changes already achieved and substantial structural reform in place, those sequencing arguments that favor structural reform first may now be satisfied, setting the scene for further disinflation. And given that successful transition may entail currencies that appreciate in real terms and rela-

tively large current account deficits—trends normally associated with weak policies—low and falling inflation may help to sustain investor confidence and the associated capital inflows.

Finally, there is no statistical evidence that the costs of disinflation are generally significant in transition economies, even at moderate inflation levels. This echoes findings for market economies (Ghosh and Phillips, 1998). And even if persistent moderate inflation has increased inflation inertia, rapid productivity growth should diminish the impact on profitability and employment of any inertia there may be in nominal wages during disinflation (Deppler, 1998).

Countries with persistent moderate inflation, as well as other advanced transition countries, now enjoy almost ideal circumstances for low-cost disinflation and would benefit from lowering inflation further. The commitment of many of them to achieving industrial country inflation rates in the near future in the context of entry to the European Union is appropriate, and others should be no less ambitious about their inflation goals.

Appendix I Relation Between Inflation and Output in Transition Revisited

Christoffersen and Doyle (1998) recently published new panel data estimates of the relationship between GDP growth and inflation in 22 transition economies between 1990 and 1997. They aimed to address three key shortcomings of the existing research. First, the collapse of major export markets was clearly key for a number of BRO countries, but it had been ignored. Second, econometric studies had not attempted to identify if disinflation had compounded output declines, as many feared would happen at the time. Third, the earlier studies imposed the assumption that inflation impairs output at all rates, rather than only above a threshold. Empirical literature on market economies has found that this understates the output costs of high inflation and overstates those of low inflation. Sarel (1996), using a panel of industrial and developing countries, finds that inflation above 8 percent significantly impedes growth, while growth is unaffected by inflation below that; Ghosh and Phillips (1998) also find a significant threshold, which they estimate in the low single digits.[26] Using the same functional form to model the threshold, the authors sought to identify if similar results held in the transition context.

Econometric Estimates

Data and Variable Construction

The panel is unbalanced, and the longest series runs from 1990–97. Christoffersen and Doyle obtained annual real GDP data, population, and the share of exports in GDP from IMF desk officers (with their estimates for 1997), data on the transition reform index from De Melo and others (1997), and updated it using the data from EBRD transition reports, and information on the direction of trade to 1996 from the Direction of Trade Statistics of the IMF. A war dummy was kindly provided by Berg and others (1998), and is described in their paper. Following Sarel (1996), two negative 12-month in-

flation rates were converted into small positive numbers to allow logs to be taken.

The export market growth series for each country in the panel was constructed as follows. Three export markets were defined: the Central and Eastern European countries; the Baltics, Russia, and other countries of the former Soviet Union; and the rest of the world. The growth of each as an export market was represented by the growth of its GDP. These growth rates were weighted according to the share of each in the exports of goods for each country in the panel. That share was taken from the earliest annual direction of trade statistics data available for each country in the sample from 1990 onwards.[27] The resulting export market growth series were then multiplied by the average ratio of exports to GDP for each country in the panel to control for openness.

Several approaches to estimating the association between growth and disinflation were examined. Dummies were defined taking the value 1 when 12-month period end inflation fell by at least 20 percent (note, this is not percentage points) from the previous year. The exercise was repeated for inflation falling by at least 50 percent from the previous year. The former gave 84 disinflation episodes, while the latter gave 56 episodes. In a further exercise, disinflation dummies were defined according to the disinflation episodes identified by Fischer and others (1996).[28]

In all cases, these disinflation episodes were divided into episodes in the context of fixed exchange rates—defined as fixed, de facto fixed, or currency board arrangements—and other exchange rate regimes. The fixed exchange rate dummy is reported in Christoffersen and Doyle (1998). The definition of a pegged exchange rate is strict, and excludes a

---

[26]Import volume growth was not used due to weak data on this for transition countries.

[27]Where data on the shares were available over several years, the weights were defined only on the basis of the share in the first year for which data were available.

[28]In this case, when a stabilization program was reported to be implemented in the first five months of a year, one was assigned to that year. But it was assigned to the following year if the stabilization was introduced later than May. This rule was an attempt to capture possible delayed effects on disinflation on output.

number of cases where some suggest that de facto pegs were operated.[29]

All observations for Tajikistan, Turkmenistan, and Uzbekistan were discarded, either because data on the direction of trade were unavailable or because the data seemed unreliable, even by the not very exacting standards of the rest of the data set. This left a panel of 22 CEE and BRO countries.

Methodology

The dependent variable, growth per capita, was selected in preference to GDP levels on the grounds that unrecorded activity may affect officially reported output levels more than growth rates. All regressions used 149 observations, and incorporated country fixed effects.

Sarel's (1996) approach to modeling a kinked relationship between inflation and output was adopted. Thus, two inflation terms are used: log inflation, and log inflation less a threshold. This second series is set to zero below the threshold. Ghosh and Phillips (1998) find that the log formulation of the twin inflation terms is accepted by their data, and it was adopted on that basis.

Following Sarel, the threshold in the second term was estimated using a grid search. The value of the threshold that maximizes the explanatory power (R-squared) of the overall equation determines the value of the threshold. If, after the grid search over R-squared, the second term in the regression that maximizes the explanatory power of the equation is insignificant, there is no nonlinearity apparent in the data. If, however, the second term is significant and negative, while the coefficient on log inflation is insignificant, then the threshold identifies the point above which the output costs of inflation become apparent in the data.

The assessment of output costs associated with disinflation controls for structural and other factors affecting output. The decomposition of the disinflation dummies into pegged and other exchange rate regimes allows some insight into the association between the exchange regime and the sacrifice ratio (the percentage loss of output per each point of reduction in inflation).

The first step was to replicate the key findings of the earlier work, and, if possible, encompass it. The second step was to investigate how disinflation affected output, as described above. Robustness tests, checking how parameter estimates were effected by inflation outliers, and by the exclusion of countries one at a time from the panel are reported in Christoffersen and Doyle (1998).

Results (1): Replication and Encompassing

GDP growth per capita was regressed on log inflation, the transition index, the change in the transition index, the war dummy, and country-specific fixed effects. The results are reported in Table 13 as regression 1. This replicates earlier findings associating low inflation and structural reform with growth (see Section III).

Then, export market growth was added to this regression, with results reported as regression 2. In this regression, inflation appears insignificant, while export market growth appears highly significant and powerful. This suggests that the earlier results concerning inflation may have been distorted by the omission of the export market growth variable.

To complete the encompassing exercise, we then added the term for log inflation less log threshold to regression 2. This is reported as regression 3.[30]

The key results are:

- Export market growth, adjusted for the share of exports in GDP, is significant at the 1 percent level, and is strongly associated with growth;
- The inflation-output threshold appears at 13 percent. The output losses associated with inflation above that level are significant at just above the 1 percent level and the term on log inflation is positive but insignificant;
- The transition index is significant at the 1 percent level and is strongly associated with growth, though not as strongly as is implied in regression 1;
- The estimate on the change in the transition index is negative, is highly significant, and is large, though not as large as in regression 1;
- The war dummy is significant at 1 percent, and is large; and
- The range of individual country error terms is large. For example, Georgia and Armenia have large negative errors in years of conflict, as do Albania, Bulgaria, and Romania in 1996–97 during the financial crises in those years.

Hence, regression 3 encompasses the earlier findings in regard to the effect of inflation on output. It also suggests lower output costs from the change in

---

[29]Fischer and others (1998) suggest that de facto pegs operated as of 1995 in Armenia, Azerbaijan, Georgia, Kazakhstan, and the Kyrgyz Republic during the sharp disinflations in that year. However, while nominal bilateral exchange rates with the U.S. dollar were relatively stable in these cases during 1995, they moved markedly in all cases except Georgia thereafter.

[30]If the primary balance of general government is included in this regression, the parameter estimate is small and positive, but statistically significant. However, it was excluded on the grounds that it is misspecified and is therefore difficult to interpret economically.

Table 13. Regression Results

Regression	1	2	3	4	5	6	7	8
The dependent variable is the percentage growth rate of GDP per capita. The p-values use White heteroskedasticity consistent standard errors and covariance.								
Independent variables								
I inflation	−0.93	−0.31	1.25	1.74	1.24	1.26	0.84	0.87
p-value	(0.077)	(0.537)	(0.100)	(0.020)	(0.105)	(0.090)	(0.240)	(0.237)
I inflation - I threshold			−2.00	−2.28	−2.04	−2.06	−1.56	−1.64
p-value			(0.017)	(0.006)	(0.016)	(0.013)	(0.076)	(0.047)
ExMkGr		2.50	2.44	2.38	2.41	2.45	2.47	2.44
p-value		(0.000)	(0.000)	(0.000)	(0.000)	(0.000)	(0.000)	(0.000)
Transition	2.98	2.31	2.09	2.03	2.11	2.09	1.98	2.01
p-value	(0.000)	(0.000)	(0.001)	(0.001)	(0.001)	(0.001)	(0.002)	(0.002)
Change transition	−2.17	−1.47	−1.42	−1.42	−1.39	−1.19	−1.41	−1.38
p-value	(0.000)	(0.007)	(0.008)	(0.009)	(0.014)	(0.060)	(0.013)	(0.008)
War	−14.1	−13.7	−14.3	−14.0	−14.4	−14.8	−14.9	−14.9
p-value	(0.003)	(0.003)	(0.003)	(0.003)	(0.002)	(0.002)	(0.002)	(0.002)
Disinflation (>20 percent)				1.21				
p-value				(0.306)				
Disinflation (>50 percent)					−0.45			
p-statistics					(0.729)			
Disinflation (Fischer)						−1.76		
p-statistics						(0.303)		
Disinflation (>50 percent, peg)							−3.63	−3.70
p-value							(0.040)	(0.037)
Disinflation (>50 percent, other)							0.48	
p-value							(0.766)	
Inflation threshold			13.0	5.0	13.0	14.0	13.0	13.0
Number of inflation observations below the threshold			36	10	36	40	36	36
Adjusted R-squared	0.612	0.647	0.652	0.651	0.649	0.652	0.652	0.654
Standard error	6.746	6.435	6.395	6.403	6.419	6.392	6.390	6.366

Source: Christoffersen and Doyle (1998).

the transition index and a weaker relationship between the level of the transition index and growth than is implied by the approach adopted by earlier researchers. Hence, the short-run output costs and long-run benefits of structural reform, while substantial, appear to be lower than earlier reported.

Results (2): Impact of Disinflation on Output

The various disinflation dummies were added in turn to regression 3.

First, the disinflation dummy for a decline of more than a fifth in the 12-month rate of inflation, along with its one-year lag, were added to regression 3. The latter was insignificant and was dropped. The regression was then rerun, and is reported as regression 4. This suggests no evidence of output loss arising from disinflation, either in the year that disinflation occurs or the following year.

When the dummy was split into episodes with fixed exchange rates and other regimes, and the regressions rerun, both dummies had insignificant coefficients.

This exercise was repeated for disinflations where inflation more than halved in one year. The results are reported as regression 5. Again, the estimate is insignificant, though eliminating the slower disinflations (of between 20 percent and 50 percent) has changed the sign on the parameter to negative. The results using the Fischer and others (1996) disinflation dummy are reported as equation 6. Again, there is no significant evidence of output loss associated with these disinflations.

When we split the dummy for disinflations of more than half into pegged and other exchange rate regimes, however, significant and large output losses were found in the presence of exchange rate pegs. This result is reported as regression 7. This regression was rerun eliminating the "nonpeg" dummy. The results are reported as regression 8.

As a final exercise, the dummies for disinflations of more than one-half were decomposed by the inflation rate being stabilized. Thus, the disinflation dummies were decomposed by prior year inflation: the first dummy included all disinflations of prior year inflation of more than 10 percent, the second included all disinflations of prior year inflation of more than 25 percent, and dummies for prior year inflation of more than 50 percent, more than 100 percent, and more than 500 percent were also formed. Regression 8 was rerun with each of these dummies included one at a time, with each dummy decomposed into pegged and other exchange rate regimes. In all cases, the nonpegged dummy was insignificant and was eliminated. The results from all the regressions indicated that as the prior year inflation cutoff increases, the negative output effects associated with pegged exchange rates decline sharply, becoming insignificant for stabilizations of inflation above 500 percent. This implies that the output losses during disinflations with pegged exchange rates tended to occur most with disinflations of more moderate inflation.

On this evidence, rapid stabilization in the presence of pegs has been associated with a large loss of output that is not accounted for by other regressors, except where high inflation was stabilized. Equally rapid stabilization of similar inflation rates under other monetary regimes has not been associated with a similar loss of output.

Discussion and Assessment

Export-Market Growth

The association of export-market growth weighted with output is marked and robust. Given the dominant role of Russia as an export market for many of the BRO countries, these findings reflect the importance of developments there for many countries in transition. Earlier studies failed to reflect this feature of transition, and as a result, misspecified the relationship between inflation and output. This omission also causes the short-run output costs of structural reform and its long-run benefits to be overstated.

Structural Reform

Notwithstanding the importance of external developments, there is evidence of a strong positive association between progress in transition and output growth, though structural reform is associated with immediate output losses.

Inflation

Evidence is found of loss of output at inflation rates above the threshold that is estimated in the low teens for the full sample, but at somewhat higher rates when the inflation outliers are excluded. As reported in the Appendix Table, one-fourth of the inflation observations occur below the estimated threshold. Accordingly, the estimate is not simply the artifact of a small number of low-inflation observations. However, the procedure does not define the confidence intervals around the identified threshold, and this counsels against overemphasis on the particular number identified as the threshold.

For the full panel, the output losses associated with inflation above the threshold are lower than has been found in other studies of transition as well as for market economies. For the latter, Sarel (1996) finds that doubling inflation, above the threshold, reduces GDP growth by 1.7 percentage points; and Ghosh and Phillips (1998) find it reduces growth by 0.5 percentage points. In contrast, these results for the full panel imply that doubling inflation above the threshold is associated with reduced growth of 0.2 percentage points. While inflation outliers and measurement problems with stockbuilding may be downwardly biasing this estimate, it is not economically negligible. Recall that Russia halved inflation seven times, and Armenia nine times between the peak and end-1997 inflation rates. Disinflation on this scale is associated with a boost to annual GDP growth rates of 1.4 percentage points and 1.8 percentage points, respectively, according to this estimate.

These findings—on the output costs of inflation above the inflation-output threshold and on the level of the threshold—should be interpreted with considerable care, however. First, correlation is not causation. While there are output costs of inflation, output can also affect inflation through the output gap and political economy factors. Second, even if the correlation does reflect causation from inflation to output, these estimates could understate the output costs of inflation now. These estimates reflect the average behavior of transition economies since 1990, and the output costs of inflation may have been rising over time. Planning mechanisms, still in place early in the panel, made poor use of information on relative prices. This suggests that when inflation obscured this information, the associated output losses were relatively low. Any losses that occurred may also have been offset if inflation eased growth-boosting relative price changes in the presence of downward nominal rigidities. But with planning mechanisms now absent and the largest of the one-off relative price changes completed, the output cost of inflation may be higher than it was on average in the period covered by the panel. For these reasons, as transition takes root, these economies could be expected to behave more like other market economies, including exhibiting greater output costs from inflation and having lower thresholds above which output costs of inflation begin to appear.

Disinflation

No systematic evidence that disinflation was associated with declines in output was found. The low inertia of inflation and the determination of the country authorities to stabilize extremely high inflation contributed to making the stabilizations highly credible, when undertaken. Even disinflations of moderate inflation do not generally appear to have incurred output costs, possibly because labor productivity and real wages are often rising rapidly, providing an ideal context for further stabilization (Deppler, 1998). There is no general evidence here to suggest that the output costs of further disinflation now would outweigh the case for further reductions in inflation.

The only evidence found of output costs from disinflation arose when moderate inflation was more than halved in the presence of pegged exchange rates. Interpreting this result is not straightforward. Output losses would occur during disinflation from moderate inflation with overdepreciated pegs. In such circumstances, stabilization would normally be expected to fail (and hence would not be picked up by the disinflation dummies) because the domestic price level would rise to eliminate the undervaluation. Only if policy directly counteracted this response, by inducing a recession, would pegs be associated both with disinflation and with output losses. This combination of outcomes seems less likely for stabilizations of high inflation with pegged exchange rates. In these cases, inflation could still fall sharply (by more than one-half), while remaining sufficiently above partner country levels to correct the undervaluation in the peg, without the need for a fall in output to render disinflation consistent with this.

On this interpretation, output losses are not due to pegs per se, but reflect the rate of inflation being stabilized, the rate at which pegs are set, and the supporting policies. Perhaps significant output losses are found because a number of stabilizations with formally pegged exchange rates were undervalued. However, it proved impossible to test this interpretation of the results directly for lack of a tractable data set on the extent of undervaluation of exchange rates.

War

There is evidence that the simple dummy for war is insufficient. Restricting conflicts to have the same impact on output is a strong assumption, and it is not even always clear when conflicts are affecting activity. For example, on the one hand, Bulgaria suffered heavily from the blockade of the former Yugoslav Republic Macedonia during that country's conflict, without itself being drawn into the conflict.[31] On the other hand, Albania may have accrued substantial rents by violating that blockade. The individual country error terms and the robustness tests suggest that the data reject the assumptions underlying the war dummy, even though they find that overall, war is highly costly. While the war dummy may be less innocent than it appears, the robustness tests suggest that its problems do not appear to be distorting the estimates of other parameters greatly.

---

[31]We are indebted to Luc Everaert for pointing this case out to us.

Appendix II   Financial Stability

Summary

Staff studies indicate that financial soundness is improving in most transition countries, though in only a few cases is the situation now comfortable. A staff study of overall Baltics, Russia, and other countries of the former Soviet Union country rankings for bank supervision places Belarus, Tajikistan, and Ukraine in the countries that have made least progress. These countries have also made least progress on bank restructuring, along with Turkmenistan and Uzbekistan. The report places all other countries into "moderate progress" and "substantial progress" groups. In the Central and Eastern European countries, the financial systems are generally most robust in moderate inflation countries, and weakest in countries with high or low inflation. This could be coincidental—moderate inflaters, such as the Czech Republic, Hungary, and Poland, have implemented more vigorous banking reforms.

Despite this progress, the soundness of the banking system remains a cause for concern for the medium-term inflation outlook. Most transition countries occupy the broad middle ground between achieving international standards of financial soundness and outright financial collapse. Further progress is needed. Moreover, assessments of financial fragility based on summary statistics are inevitably subject to major qualifications. Summary statistics, including risk-weighted capital and nonperforming credits, can mislead when accounting practices, supervision, and legislation are lacking; it is difficult to assess interest, exchange rate, or market risks at an aggregate level, though these risks may be particularly high in a transition environment where many financial institutions may be unfamiliar with them.

The Baltics, Russia, and Other Countries of the Former Soviet Union

A study prepared by IMF staff for the group of central banks providing technical assistance to transition countries concludes that since commencing transition, all the Baltics, Russia, and other countries of the former Soviet Union, except Tajikistan, have developed at least "adequate" prudential regulations, though some countries, such as Estonia, surpass this minimal standard. However, in important areas, including corrective action and market exit, implementation is still generally lacking.

There has been good progress in building bank supervisory capacity in Armenia, the Baltics, Kazakhstan, the Kyrgyz Republic, Moldova, and Russia, including the increase in numbers of supervisory staff in all Baltics, Russia, and other countries of the former Soviet Union, except Belarus. The key remaining supervisory weakness identified is the absence of clear accounting rules—on consolidation of balance sheets, rules for loan classification, loan-loss provisioning, and income recognition—the consequences of which include compromised off-site supervision.[32]

Bank restructuring, however, remains urgent. Of the Baltics, Russia, and other countries of the former Soviet Union with international accounting standards, the median ratio of nonperforming loans to total loans is estimated at 18 percent, and the largest share of bad debts is concentrated in large—often former state-owned—banks that dominate their banking systems. Many new private banks are also in difficulty due to poor management. Nonetheless, progress has been made. While the number of banks remained broadly unchanged in the Kyrgyz Republic, Latvia, Lithuania, Moldova, Turkmenistan, and Ukraine, 13 percent of banks in the Baltics, Russia, and other countries of the former Soviet Union were closed during 1996; the number increased only in Tajikistan. Formal restructuring strategies have been developed in Azerbaijan, Georgia, Kazakhstan, the Kyrgyz Republic, and Moldova. Others, including Armenia, Tajikistan, and Russia, are proceeding on a more ad hoc basis. Russia is focusing on strengthen-

---

[32]Other deficiencies noted include the following: seven countries had not introduced internationally acceptable accounting standards for commercial banks by 1997; Belarus, Moldova, and Russia had not yet introduced consolidated supervision; there were no limits on equity participation of banks in Moldova, Tajikistan, and Turkmenistan; and licensing procedures needed close surveillance, especially in Belarus and Tajikistan.

ing its capacity to monitor its largest banks, which, unusually, are mostly new commercial banks.

Central and Eastern European Countries

The Macedonian and Slovenian authorities are alone in initiating efforts to address financial fragility as part of their disinflation programs, though the problems in the former case were also particularly severe. The Macedonian authorities recapitalized Stopanska Banka, which accounted for a little under half of deposits in the banking system; they assumed all Paris and London Club debt; and they assumed all households' foreign currency deposits. But M2 was only just over 10 percent of GDP, which limited the threat to disinflation posed by financial fragility. Following disinflation, Stopanska Banka continues to absorb public resources, but its bad debts, like those elsewhere in the banking system, are fully provisioned. Financial sector policy is now focused on stimulating growth and competition, and strengthening the financial sector. In Slovenia, bank rehabilitation dates from late 1991, in respect of the three most troubled banks, which held 65 percent of banking sector assets, but the procedure was not completed until 1997. Upgrading financial sector legislation has been similarly protracted, with the focus now on meeting EU norms. Banks report capital of over 20 percent of risk-weighted assets, with bad debts well below 10 percent of credit, but the authorities consider these data to be somewhat over optimistic.

In the Central and Eastern European countries, major restructuring of the banking systems in Hungary and Poland during the mid-1990s led to sharp reductions in the share of nonperforming loans in bank portfolios to 14 percent in Poland, and 11½ percent in Hungary at the end of 1996. In Poland, some progress has been made to privatize the banking system, while in Hungary, this progress has been even more marked. Hungary maintains capital and reserves well over double the Basle minimum risk-weighted capital adequacy guideline and nearly double the minimum guideline of 12 percent for developing countries.

While nonperforming loans in the Czech and Slovak Republics have also declined relative to credit, they remained at just below 30 percent in 1997, and at about one-third in the largest banks that dominate both financial systems. In the Czech Republic, this reflects both the slow growth of overall credit and the deliberately limited adoption of bad debts by the state. As a result, bank capital is only marginally above the Basle minimum guideline and is below the guideline

for developing countries, and bank profitability is low and falling. In Slovakia, the three largest banks have capital of below 5 percent of risk-weighted assets, though smaller banks are usually well above the 8 percent minimum. Efforts to strengthen the regulatory framework and to privatize the main banks have recently been accelerated in the Czech Republic.

Several regional banks in Croatia suffered badly during the hostilities, and restructuring did not start in earnest until late 1995, well after disinflation. Several banks have been recapitalized, and the restructuring of the major troubled bank, Privredna Banka, which held about 20 percent of deposits in 1996, has thus far included recapitalization and bad debt write-offs. As a result, banks report capital in 1996 of just below 20 percent of risk-weighted assets, but there are considerable doubts about the accounting practices underlying these data. Efforts to strengthen banking supervision and accounting regulations continue.

In the three cases where disinflation has been reversed—Albania, Bulgaria after the first stabilization, and Romania—financial fragility has been severe. In Romania, while the banking legislative infrastructure is generally appropriate and most banks report capital in excess of the Basle minimum guideline, implementation and enforcement have been weak. By the end of 1995, nonperforming loans had risen to 35 percent of credit, underprovisioning was substantial, and pyramid schemes have flourished and (inevitably) collapsed. Two bank failures in 1996 highlighted these weaknesses and led to a relaxation of monetary policy.

In Bulgaria, a pervasive "soft-budget" constraint culture culminated in banking crisis in 1996, and in hyperinflation in early 1997. Poor lending throughout the 1990s led to negative net worth of the banking system estimated by the IMF at 10 percent of GDP in 1995, with 75 percent of loans nonperforming at that time. Attempts to avert a loss of confidence in banks from late 1995, including management changes, a new deposit insurance scheme, and bank closures, failed. Widespread runs on banks ensued, and subsequent bank closures accounted for just below 30 percent of bank deposits. However, only relatively healthy banks have survived, so the system is now considerably stronger. In Albania, 27 percent of loans made in the 18 months to the end of 1994 (post-transition) were nonperforming, in addition to the much larger nonperforming portfolio that commercial banks inherited. Initiatives to privatize the state-owned banks have made little headway in practice, and, in this environment, an informal market, including pyramid schemes, flourished. The latter collapsed spectacularly from the end of 1996 amid riots, causing a sharp depreciation in the currency. By September 1997, 39 percent of loans by state-owned banks were nonperforming.

References

Amsden, Alice H., Jacek Kochanowicz, and Lance Taylor, 1994, *The Market Meets Its Match: Restructuring the Economies of Eastern Europe* (Cambridge, Massachusetts: Harvard University Press).

Anderson, Jonathan, and Daniel A. Citrin, 1995, "The Behavior of Inflation and Velocity," in *Policy Experiences and Issues in the Baltics, Russia, and Other Countries of the Former Soviet Union,* edited by Daniel A. Citrin and Ashok K. Lahiri, IMF Occasional Paper 133 (Washington: International Monetary Fund).

Åslund, Anders, Peter Boone, and Simon Johnson, 1996, "How to Stabilize: Lessons from Post-Communist Countries," *Brookings Papers on Economic Activity,* No. 1, pp. 217–313.

Ball, Lawrence, and N. Gregory Mankiw, 1994, "Asymmetric Price Adjustment and Economic Fluctuations," *The Economic Journal,* Vol. 104, pp. 247–61.

Begg, David, 1998, "Disinflation in Central and Eastern Europe: The Experience to Date," in *Moderate Inflation: The Experience of Transition Economies,* edited by Carlo Cottarelli and György Szapáry (Washington: International Monetary Fund and National Bank of Hungary).

———, L. Hesselman, and R. Smith, 1996, "Money in Transition: How Much Do We Know?" (mimeo; International Monetary Fund).

Berg, Andrew, Eduardo Borensztein, Ratna Sahay, and Jeromin Zettlemeyer, 1998, "The Evolution of Output in Transition Economies: Explaining the Differences" (mimeo; International Monetary Fund).

Blanchard, Olivier, 1998, "The Optimal Speed of Disinflation: The Case of Hungary," in *Moderate Inflation: The Experience of Transition Economies,* edited by Carlo Cottarelli and György Szapáry (Washington: International Monetary Fund and National Bank of Hungary).

Bruno, Michael, 1992, "Stabilization and Reform in Eastern Europe—A Preliminary Evaluation," *Staff Papers,* International Monetary Fund, Vol. 39 (December), pp. 741–77.

———, 1996, *Deep Crises and Reform: What Have We Learned?* (Washington: World Bank).

———, and William Easterly, 1995, "Inflation Crises and Long-Run Growth," NBER Working Paper 5209 (Cambridge, Massachusetts: National Bureau of Economic Research).

Budina, Nina, and Sweder van Wijnbergen, 1997, "Fiscal Policies in Eastern Europe," *Oxford Review of Economic Policy,* Vol. 13, No. 2, pp. 47–64.

Buiter, Willem H., 1997, "Aspects of Fiscal Performance in Some Transition Economies Under Fund-Supported Programs," IMF Working Paper 97/31 (Washington: International Monetary Fund).

Bulir, Ales, 1998, "Income Inequality: Does Inflation Matter?" IMF Working Paper 98/7 (Washington: International Monetary Fund).

Burton, David, and Stanley Fischer, 1998, "Ending Moderate Inflations," in *Moderate Inflation: The Experience of Transition Economies,* edited by Carlo Cottarelli and György Szapáry (Washington: International Monetary Fund and National Bank of Hungary).

Calvo, Guillermo A., and Fabrizio Coricelli, 1992, "Stabilizing a Previously Centrally Planned Economy: Poland 1990," *Economic Policy: A European Forum,* No. 14, pp. 175–208 and 213–26.

Cangiano, Marco, Carlo Cottarelli, and Luis Cubeddu, 1998, *Pension Developments and Reform in Transition Economies,* paper presented at the conference on Social Security Reforms: International Comparisons, held in Rome, March 16–17, 1998.

Christoffersen, Peter, and Peter Doyle, 1998, "From Inflation to Growth: Eight Years of Transition," IMF Working Paper 98/99 (Washington: International Monetary Fund).

Coorey, Sharmini, Mauro Mecagni, and Erik Offerdal, 1998, "Disinflation in Transition Economies: The Role of Relative Price Adjustment," in *Moderate Inflation: The Experience of Transition Economies,* edited by Carlo Cottarelli and György Szapáry (Washington: International Monetary Fund and National Bank of Hungary).

Cottarelli, Carlo, and Curzio Giannini, 1997, *Credibility Without Rules? Monetary Frameworks in the Post-Bretton Woods Era,* IMF Occasional Paper 154 (Washington: International Monetary Fund).

Cottarelli, Carlo, Mark Griffiths, and Reza Moghadam, 1998, "The Nonmonetary Determinants of Inflation," IMF Working Paper 98/23 (Washington: International Monetary Fund).

Cottarelli, Carlo, and György Szapáry, eds., 1998, *Moderate Inflation: The Experience of Transition Economies* (Washington: International Monetary Fund and National Bank of Hungary).

Cukierman, Alex, 1992, *Central Bank Strategy, Credibility, and Independence: Theory and Evidence* (Cambridge, Massachusetts: MIT Press).

———, Geoffrey P. Miller, and Bilin Neyapti, 1998, *Central Bank Reform, Liberalization and Inflation in Transi-*

tion Economies—An International Perspective (mimeo; Tel Aviv University, Israel).

De Broeck, Mark, Kornélia Krajnyák, and Henri Lorie, 1997, "Explaining and Forecasting the Velocity of Money in Transition Economies, with Special Reference to the Baltics, Russia, and Other Countries of the Former Soviet Union," IMF Working Paper 97/108 (Washington: International Monetary Fund).

De Melo, Martha, Cevdet Denizer, and Alan Gelb, 1997, "From Plan to Market: Patterns of Transition," in *Macroeconomic Stabilization in Transition Economies,* edited by Mario J. Blejer and Marko Škreb (Cambridge, United Kingdom: Cambridge University Press).

Deppler, Michael, 1998, "Is Reducing Moderate Inflation Costly?" in *Moderate Inflation: The Experience of Transition Economies,* edited by Carlo Cottarelli and György Szapáry (Washington: International Monetary Fund and National Bank of Hungary).

Dornbusch, Rudiger, 1976, "Expectations and Exchange Rate Dynamics," *Journal of Political Economy,* Vol. 84, pp. 1161–76.

European Bank for Reconstruction and Development, 1997, *Transition Report* (London: EBRD).

Fedorov, Boris, 1995, "Macroeconomic Policy and Stabilization in Russia," in *Russian Economic Reform at Risk,* edited by Anders Åslund (New York: Pinter).

Fischer, Stanley, Ratna Sahay, and Carlos A. Végh, 1996, "Stabilization and Growth in Transition Economies: The Early Experience," *Journal of Economic Perspectives,* Vol. 10, No. 2, pp. 45–66.

———, 1998, "From Transition to Market: Evidence and Growth Prospects," IMF Working Paper 98/52 (Washington: International Monetary Fund).

Ghosh, Atish, R., 1997, "Inflation in Transition Economies: How Much? And Why?" IMF Working Paper 97/80 (Washington: International Monetary Fund).

———, and Steven Phillips, 1998, "Inflation, Disinflation, and Growth," IMF Working Paper 98/68 (Washington: International Monetary Fund).

Gomulka, Stanislaw, 1998, "A Comment on David Begg," in *Moderate Inflation: The Experience of Transition Economies,* edited by Carlo Cottarelli and György Szapáry (Washington: International Monetary Fund and National Bank of Hungary).

Hansson, Ardo, H., 1997, "Macroeconomic Stabilization in the Baltic States," in *Macroeconomic Stabilization in Transition Economies,* edited by Mario J. Blejer and Marko Škreb (Cambridge, United Kingdom: Cambridge University Press).

Hendry, David, 1995, *Dynamic Econometrics* (New York: Oxford University Press).

Hernandez-Catá, Ernesto, forthcoming, "Price Liberalization, Money Growth, and Inflation During the Transition to a Market Economy" (Washington: International Monetary Fund).

International Monetary Fund, 1997, *World Economic Outlook,* Chapter V (Washington), pp. 98–118.

———, 1998, *Status of Market-Based Central Banking Reforms in the Baltics, Russia, and Other Countries of the Former Soviet Union,* report prepared for the Eleventh Coordination Meeting of Cooperating Central Banks and International Institutions (Washington: International Monetary Fund).

Knight, Malcolm, 1997, *Central Bank Reforms in the Baltics, Russia, and the Other Countries of the Former Soviet Union,* IMF Occasional Paper 157 (Washington: International Monetary Fund).

Koen, Vincent, and Paula R. De Masi, 1997, "Prices in the Transition: Ten Stylized Facts," in *Staff Studies for the World Economic Outlook* (Washington: International Monetary Fund).

Kornai, János, 1998, "Comments on the Appropriate Speed of Disinflation," in *Moderate Inflation: The Experience of Transition Economies,* edited by Carlo Cottarelli and György Szapáry (Washington: International Monetary Fund and National Bank of Hungary).

Krajnyák, Kornélia, and Christoph Klingen, 1998, *Price Adjustment and Inflation in the Baltics, 1993–96* (mimeo; International Monetary Fund).

Lougani, Prakash, and Nathan Sheets, 1997, "Central Bank Independence, Inflation, and Growth in Transition Economies," *Journal of Money, Credit, and Banking,* Vol. 29, No. 3 (August), pp. 381–99.

Mackenzie, George A., and Peter Stella, 1996, *Quasi-Fiscal Operations and Public Financial Institutions,* IMF Occasional Paper 142 (Washington: International Monetary Fund).

Masson, Paul, Miguel A. Savastano, and Sunil Sharma, 1997, "The Scope for Inflation Targeting in Developing Countries," IMF Working Paper 97/130 (Washington: International Monetary Fund).

Medgyessy, Peter, 1998, "Introductory Remarks," in *Moderate Inflation: The Experience of Transition Economies,* edited by Carlo Cottarelli and György Szapáry (Washington: International Monetary Fund and National Bank of Hungary).

Morsink, James H.J., 1995, "Wage Controls during IMF Arrangements in Central Europe," in *IMF Conditionality: Experience Under Stand-By and Extended Arrangements,* by Susan Schadler and others, IMF Occasional Paper 129 (Washington: International Monetary Fund).

Nuxoll, Daniel, 1996, *The Convergence of Price Structures and Economic Growth,* paper presented at the NBER Conference on Research in Income and Wealth, Arlington, Virginia, March 15–16.

Portes, Richard, editor, 1993, *Economic Transformation in Central Europe: A Progress Report* (London: Centre for Economic Policy Research).

Pujol, Thierry, and Mark Griffiths, 1998, "Moderate Inflation in Poland: A Real Story," in *Moderate Inflation: The Experience of Transition Economies,* edited by Carlo Cottarelli and György Szapáry (Washington: International Monetary Fund and National Bank of Hungary).

Radzyner, Olga, and Sandra Riesinger, 1997, "Central Bank Independence in Transition: Legislation and Reality in Central and Eastern Europe," *Focus on Transition,* Vol. 2, No. 2, pp. 57–90.

Richards, Anthony, and Gunnar Tersman, 1995, "Growth, Nontradeables, and Price Convergence in the Baltics,"

IMF Working Paper 95/45 (Washington: International Monetary Fund).

Rosenberg, Christoph, B., and Tapio O. Saavalainen, 1998, "How to Deal with Azerbaijan's Oil Boom? Policy Strategies in a Resource-Rich Transition Economy," IMF Working Paper 98/6 (Washington: International Monetary Fund).

Ross, Kevin, 1998, "Post Stabilization Inflation Dynamics in Slovenia," IMF Working Paper 98/27 (Washington: International Monetary Fund).

Sarel, Michael, 1996, "Nonlinear Effects of Inflation on Economic Growth," *Staff Papers,* International Monetary Fund, Vol. 43 (March), pp. 199–215.

Sargent, Thomas J., and Neil Wallace, 1981, "Some Unpleasant Monetary Arithmetic," *Federal Reserve Bank of Minneapolis Quarterly Review* (Fall), pp. 1–17.

Selgin, George, 1994, "On Ensuring the Acceptability of a New Fiat Money," *Journal of Money, Credit, and Banking,* Vol. 26 (November), pp. 808–26.

Škreb, Marko, "A Note on Inflation," 1998, in *Moderate Inflation: The Experience of Transition Economies,* edited by Carlo Cottarelli and György Szapáry (Washington: International Monetary Fund and National Bank of Hungary).

Surányi, György, and János Vincze, 1998, "Inflation in Hungary (1990–97)," in *Moderate Inflation: The Experience of Transition Economies,* edited by Carlo Cottarelli and György Szapáry (Washington: International Monetary Fund and National Bank of Hungary).

Szapáry, György, 1998, "Disinflation Policies: Issues of Sequencing," in *Moderate Inflation: The Experience of Transition Economies,* edited by Carlo Cottarelli and György Szapáry (Washington: International Monetary Fund and National Bank of Hungary).

Van Elkan, Rachel, 1998, "How Stable Is Money Demand?" in *Hungary: Economic Policies for Sustainable Growth,* by Carlo Cottarelli and others, IMF Occasional Paper 159 (Washington: International Monetary Fund).

Woźniak, Przemystaw, 1998, "Relative Price Adjustment in Poland, Hungary and the Czech Republic. Comparison of the Size and Impact on Inflation," CASE-CEV, Working Paper Series, Budapest.

Zavoico, Basil, 1995, *A Brief Note on the Inflationary Process in Transition Economies* (mimeo; International Monetary Fund).

Zettermeyer, Jeromin, and Daniel A. Citrin, 1995, "Stabilization: Fixed Versus Flexible Exchange Rates," in *Policy Experiences and Issues in the Baltics, Russia, and Other Countries of the Former Soviet Union,* edited by Daniel A. Citrin and Ashok K. Lahiri, IMF Occasional Paper 133 (Washington: International Monetary Fund).

Recent Occasional Papers of the International Monetary Fund

157. Central Bank Reforms in the Baltics, Russia, and the Other Countries of the Former Soviet Union, by a staff team led by Malcolm Knight and comprising Susana Almuiña, John Dalton, Inci Otker, Ceyla Pazarbaşıoğlu, Arne B. Petersen, Peter Quirk, Nicholas M. Roberts, Gabriel Sensenbrenner, and Jan Willem van der Vossen. 1997.

156. The ESAF at Ten Years: Economic Adjustment and Reform in Low-Income Countries, by the staff of the International Monetary Fund. 1997.

155. Fiscal Policy Issues During the Transition in Russia, by Augusto Lopez-Claros and Sergei V. Alexashenko. 1998.

154. Credibility Without Rules? Monetary Frameworks in the Post–Bretton Woods Era, by Carlo Cottarelli and Curzio Giannini. 1997.

153. Pension Regimes and Saving, by G.A. Mackenzie, Philip Gerson, and Alfredo Cuevas. 1997.

152. Hong Kong, China: Growth, Structural Change, and Economic Stability During the Transition, by John Dodsworth and Dubravko Mihaljek. 1997.

151. Currency Board Arrangements: Issues and Experiences, by a staff team led by Tomás J.T. Baliño and Charles Enoch. 1997.

150. Kuwait: From Reconstruction to Accumulation for Future Generations, by Nigel Andrew Chalk, Mohamed A. El-Erian, Susan J. Fennell, Alexei P. Kireyev, and John F. Wilson. 1997.

149. The Composition of Fiscal Adjustment and Growth: Lessons from Fiscal Reforms in Eight Economies, by G.A. Mackenzie, David W.H. Orsmond, and Philip R. Gerson. 1997.

148. Nigeria: Experience with Structural Adjustment, by Gary Moser, Scott Rogers, and Reinold van Til, with Robin Kibuka and Inutu Lukonga. 1997.

147. Aging Populations and Public Pension Schemes, by Sheetal K. Chand and Albert Jaeger. 1996.

146. Thailand: The Road to Sustained Growth, by Kalpana Kochhar, Louis Dicks-Mireaux, Balazs Horvath, Mauro Mecagni, Erik Offerdal, and Jianping Zhou. 1996.

145. Exchange Rate Movements and Their Impact on Trade and Investment in the APEC Region, by Takatoshi Ito, Peter Isard, Steven Symansky, and Tamim Bayoumi. 1996.

144. National Bank of Poland: The Road to Indirect Instruments, by Piero Ugolini. 1996.

143. Adjustment for Growth: The African Experience, by Michael T. Hadjimichael, Michael Nowak, Robert Sharer, and Amor Tahari. 1996.

142. Quasi-Fiscal Operations of Public Financial Institutions, by G.A. Mackenzie and Peter Stella. 1996.

141. Monetary and Exchange System Reforms in China: An Experiment in Gradualism, by Hassanali Mehran, Marc Quintyn, Tom Nordman, and Bernard Laurens. 1996.

140. Government Reform in New Zealand, by Graham C. Scott. 1996.

139. Reinvigorating Growth in Developing Countries: Lessons from Adjustment Policies in Eight Economies, by David Goldsbrough, Sharmini Coorey, Louis Dicks-Mireaux, Balazs Horvath, Kalpana Kochhar, Mauro Mecagni, Erik Offerdal, and Jianping Zhou. 1996.

138. Aftermath of the CFA Franc Devaluation, by Jean A.P. Clément, with Johannes Mueller, Stéphane Cossé, and Jean Le Dem. 1996.

137. The Lao People's Democratic Republic: Systemic Transformation and Adjustment, edited by Ichiro Otani and Chi Do Pham. 1996.

136. Jordan: Strategy for Adjustment and Growth, edited by Edouard Maciejewski and Ahsan Mansur. 1996.

135. Vietnam: Transition to a Market Economy, by John R. Dodsworth, Erich Spitäller, Michael Braulke, Keon Hyok Lee, Kenneth Miranda, Christian Mulder, Hisanobu Shishido, and Krishna Srinivasan. 1996.

134. India: Economic Reform and Growth, by Ajai Chopra, Charles Collyns, Richard Hemming, and Karen Parker with Woosik Chu and Oliver Fratzscher. 1995.

Note: For information on the title and availability of Occasional Papers not listed, please consult the IMF Publications Catalog or contact IMF Publication Services.